*"THAT'S* OUR NEW
AD CAMPAIGN . . . ?"

# "*THAT'S* OUR NEW AD CAMPAIGN . . . ?"

*A Handy Guide for CEOs, Presidents,
Ad Managers, Account Executives, Art Directors,
Copywriters, Students, and Anybody Else Who Wants
to Learn How to Create Better Ads*

Dick Wasserman

Lexington Books

D.C. Heath and Company

Lexington, Massachusetts/Toronto

The author and publisher express their thanks to those
who have granted permission to reproduce
copyrighted text. The copyright
acknowledgments appear on page xi.

**Library of Congress Cataloging-in-Publication Data**

Wasserman, Dick.
That's our new ad campaign— ?
1. Advertising campaigns—Evaluation.   I. Title.
HF5823.W417   1988      659.1'13      87-45776
ISBN 0-669-16974-9 (alk. paper)

Published simultaneously in Canada
Printed in the United States of America
International Standard Book Number: 0-669-16974-9
Library of Congress Catalog Card Number: 87-45776

The paper used in this publication meets the minimum requirements of
American National Standard for Information Sciences—Permanence
of Paper for Printed Library Materials, ANSI Z39.48-1984.

ISBN 0-669-16974-9

88 89 90 91 92 8 7 6 5 4 3 2 1

TO DOROTHY AND BEN WASSERMAN

# CONTENTS

# NOTE TO THE READER

Throughout this book, I use the phrase *ad manager* as a convenient catchall. It refers to the individual who is responsible for dealing with a client's advertising agency, evaluating its work, and selling that work to top management. In many companies, the head of sales, marketing, public relations, or corporate communications performs this function. Sometimes the company's president does it. It was much easier to write "ad manager" over and over rather than "ad, sales, or marketing manager; public relations person; or corporate communications head." I have also used the male form of the personal pronoun in most cases, again for convenience, instead of constantly writing "he or she."

# ACKNOWLEDGMENTS

My thanks to Bill Backer, Phil Dusenberry, Peter Barnet, and Murray Hysen for being so generous with their time and talent. Bob Schlesinger suggested the title. Thanks also to Bob Meury, Jack Lambert, Marty Rubin, and Marty Beim for the many hours they spent reading the manuscript and for their helpful comments and criticisms.

# PROLOGUE

———

A clever cartoon that appeared in a recent issue of *The New Yorker* showed a distinguished but somewhat befuddled speaker, in cap and gown, addressing a mass of graduating college students on a campus lawn. The caption read, "I know so much that I don't even know where to begin."

Like the speaker, when I began this book, I felt quite knowledgeable but a bit befuddled. I knew a lot about creating advertising, but although I had taught copywriting courses in college, I was not sure I knew how or where to begin teaching professional marketers how to evaluate advertising more effectively.

You do not need a Ph.D. in advertising to evaluate advertising effectively. What you need—and what most advertisers lack—is a conceptual framework. Lacking that, one person's opinion is as good or bad as another's, since everyone, including the consumer, is his own advertising expert.

Copywriters and art directors work instinctively, so even the best of them have little guidance to offer people who cannot intuitively appreciate what they do.

What I have to offer that I am convinced is unique is a conceptual framework that makes it relatively easy to judge the difference between a good and a bad piece of advertising, or, if you will, between effective and ineffective advertising. It is based on two things: the methods and techniques I developed and perfected teaching copywriting to college students for nearly ten years at the School of Visual Arts, and almost twenty-five years of copywriting experience at many of New York's best advertising agencies.

In order to make the framework I've constructed and the creative guidelines I offer more concrete, I have provided examples of more than two dozen excellent published and broadcast advertisements, along with detailed critiques of each. Working with an expert art director, I have also created ten representative examples of speculative rough (headlines and layouts) print ads that demonstrate some of the most common mistakes made by advertisers.

Even the best book can only do so much, especially in as personal and subjective an area as evaluating advertising. Learning to judge ads skillfully is, always has been, and must continue to be a hands-on experience. But this process, especially as it occurs in large corporations, is random, haphazard, and slow. I believe my book can help speed things up considerably.

My fondest hope is that in some way and to some small degree, my book will help shake up a few members of the U.S. corporate establishment. They need shaking up because, on the whole, big budget advertising in the United States, which is their responsibility, is still as low quality a product as our cars, appliances, and TV sets were a few short years ago.

The best of American advertising is equal to the best in the world. But there's not nearly enough of the best, and there's far too much of the worst. Excellent advertising is created for clients and recommended to them every day of the week. But time and time again, it is rejected by middle management or diluted by committees responsible to upper management. Or it takes top management so long to make a decision that what started out as good work becomes mediocre work because it is rushed into production too quickly at the last moment.

With a few notable exceptions, *corporate executives in America do not understand the difference between good advertising and bad advertising. Search for Excellence* author Tom Peters is right: They do not like advertising because they regard selling as a necessary evil; they feel there is something disreputable about it. They do not respect advertising people. Unlike such enlightened individuals as Colgate's chairman Reuben Marks, they treat their agencies as suppliers instead of partners because they do not trust them.

The result is that billions of dollars' worth of advertising is wasted every year in the United States. In these days of intense global competition, that's a price this nation cannot afford to pay. On the whole, our marketing machinery is still first rate in this country. It may well be the only piece of machinery we have left that's on a par with anything made in Japan. But our competitors are at the gates. They are learning quickly. Much of the advertising created in England and Europe these days is very, very good. The Asian basin nations are learning more every day. We may be able to stay ahead if, among other things, we can learn to market our goods and services more efficiently by advertising them more effectively. We must work very hard to learn as much as we can, as quickly as we can.

The hour is late.

# WE HAVE MET THE ENEMY AND HE IS US

## 1

The first thing anybody with any sense asks about the creative part of advertising is, Isn't it highly subjective?

It is.

What's worse, advertising exists more or less on the fly; it catches the public's attention or—one hopes—its fancy for a few weeks, months, or years at best, and then passes from the scene. So any sort of judgment about its effectiveness is bound to have an evanescent, will-o'-the-wisp quality.

On the other hand, the old bell-shaped curve we all learned about in college should apply to advertising just as it does to most other kinds of human endeavor. Statistically speaking, you might expect about one-sixth, or roughly 15 percent, of the advertising that's published and broadcast to be outstanding—provocative and persuasive because it's clever and innovative. Roughly 70 percent should be more or less O.K.—not necessarily great but by no means terrible. And 10 or at the most 15 percent should be so dull that few customers pay much attention to it.

If you were to ask a group of top creative adpeople to judge the ads in a national consumer magazine, you might expect their judgments to follow the bell-shaped curve. I asked six creative directors, all of them senior vice-presidents at major New York agencies, to evaluate the ads in a typical issue of *Newsweek*. There were 78 single-page, two-page spread, and quarter-page ads in this issue. I told them to presume the purpose of an ad is to attract readers' attention and persuade or convince them to buy, try, or feel more favorably disposed toward a product. "In light of that presumption," I asked, "how many of the ads in this magazine are not as effective as they could and should be?"

The most critical judge picked 36 ads as failures, the most charitable, 28. The others chose 31, 29, 32, and 34 ads as complete creative failures. Twenty-two ads appeared on everybody's list. On average, over 40 percent of the ads were judged failures. When I asked six nonprofessionals who were connected with advertising indirectly to make this same judgment, their failure score averaged over 35 percent.

I tried similar experiments a few more times. In a recent issue of one of the leading U.S. business magazines, several top creative adpeople chose an average of 59 out of 109 ads—54 percent—as, in the words of one, "so dull and boring, they're a waste of client money."

I asked another equally senior group to tell me how many ads in another consumer magazine were all they could be, in creative terms. One creative director chose only 3 out of 40, about 7.5 percent. The other chose 4, or just 10 percent. Three more creative directors judged the ads equally harshly. The totals: *From 75 to 85 percent of the ads could have been more effective.*

I asked half a dozen senior creative people to study the ads in a trade magazine, chosen at random. The question: Are there any ads in this magazine that are so dull, boring, or confusing, by your professionally acceptable standard of creativity, as to be complete failures? Of twenty-two ads in the magazine, *nobody* judged more than *four* to be up to the "minimum level of professionally acceptable creativity." In other words, no more than about 15 percent were judged acceptable. The comments on the other 85 percent ranged from "shockingly bad," "inept," and "ridiculous," to "a joke, professionally speaking."

Quoting a Harvard study in a speech to the American Association of Advertising Agencies at Pebble Beach, California, in 1962, Bill Bernbach said that 85 percent of advertising is ignored. In the ensuing twenty-six years, many of the best minds in advertising have said virtually the same thing time and time again. My admittedly small, unscientific sample seems to bear out the truth of what Bernbach said. Whether the figure is 85 or 75 or 55 or even 40 percent, it is obvious that, of the $90 billion spent on advertising in the United States every year, tens of billions of dollars, which our economic system can ill afford, are being wasted.

# BETTER TO LIGHT A CANDLE THAN CURSE THE DARKNESS—BUT SOMETIMES YOU CAN SHED A LITTLE LIGHT BY ASKING HOW IT GOT SO DARK IN THE FIRST PLACE.

> Selling—and advertising. Many [corporate executives] are as contemptuous of most advertising as they are of salesmen. Many consider it to be "mere fluff"! Most of our technical (and banking, etc.) friends hate it. Actually they resent the need for it. "It should be obvious to any fool that the benefits of these management services (of ours) are overwhelming," is the sentiment just a millimeter below the surface. They look at [advertising] not with thinly disguised contempt but with wholesale contempt.
> —Tom Peters and Nancy Austin, *A Passion For Excellence*, 1985, 92–93

There are four reasons that advertising makes businesspeople so uncomfortable. First, by its public nature advertising makes them feel exposed and vulnerable. They feel threatened in the same way they do when they face the press, only more so, because advertising bears the company's personal stamp.

Second, by nature, managers like to control everything that affects their company. But no matter how hard they try, they cannot fully control what people will think of their advertising.

Third, corporate managers are inclined toward understatement. They value calm and quiet, abhor emotional displays, and do everything possible to make decisions in a dispassionate and objective manner. Advertising rubs them the wrong way—it smacks too much of hoopla and harlequins, impulse and emotion, drama and stagecraft. It is simply too much like show business for their taste.

Fourth, and most important, although they may have read a book by an advertising luminary like David Ogilvy or Jerry Della Femina, few corporate executives have ever had the craft of admaking explained to them in a systematic way. Most have never written an ad themselves or had any formal training in admaking. They lack both a coherent, cohesive framework and a consistent set of principles against which to judge a given ad or commercial.

## PITY THE POOR ADVERTISING MANAGER

The more innately hostile toward and suspicious of advertising top managers are, the more uncomfortable and at times humiliating the position of the typical advertising manager becomes. In many cases he is treated as a distant cousin instead of a member of the immediate corporate family. His decisions are questioned, however subtly, or countermanded, or simply ignored because top management has decided it feels differently about what are "obviously" subjective creative criteria. Advertising strategies may change at a moment's notice, copy may be rewritten by the chairman or the president without explanation. The members of numerous committees may be invited to express their opinions or even to tinker directly with the advertising. Often, when ad managers try to sell the agency's creative work to top management, they feel intimidated because they sense management's alienation from and discomfort with advertising.

# LIGHTING UP THE HEART OF DARKNESS

## 2

Before your agency can create effective advertising, you and it have to put your heads together and agree on what you want to say, how often you can afford to say it, and whom you want to say it to. In other words, you have to come up with a *marketing strategy*. After that, it's up to your agency to think of ways of saying it that will attract people's attention. *What* you say—the claim you want to make or the benefit you want to call people's attention to—can be thought of as the *creative strategy*. The *way* you say it is called the *creative execution*.

The cause of all that mediocre advertising I mentioned is not faulty marketing strategies. Over time, skilled people with sufficient experience, a reasonable amount of common sense, and access to decent research can usually hammer out an effective marketing strategy. The problem is that the typical advertiser isn't very good at evaluating creative executions. In fact, most advertisers are terrible at it. It isn't that corporate presidents or ad managers are stupid. It's that nobody has ever taught them how to judge advertising. Some people feel it's the sort of thing that can only be learned on the job. But that is simply not true. During my years on the faculty of the School of Visual Arts in New York City, I

taught hundreds of young people with no advertising experience how to evaluate and create advertising. *Judging* advertising is a lot like *making* advertising,
and making advertising is like building a brick wall. Given cement, bricks, a
trowel, and enough time, most of us could create a wall of some sort. But it
wouldn't look anything like the wall a professional bricklayer would build, it
wouldn't hold up as well, and it would take a hell of a lot longer to build it. Just
as you can be taught how to build a better wall, you can be taught how to judge
advertising skillfully. All you need is the right teacher.

## THE BENEFIT: THE HEART OF ANY AD

On the whole, people buy *benefits*, not products. One way or another, ads must
hold out, directly or indirectly, the hope that the reader or viewer will derive
some advantage or improvement from reading the ad or watching the commercial or listening to the radio spot.

Some ads, such as classified ads, can be effective even though they are simple
and primitive. Classified ads identify the product or the service in the headline,
use abbreviated copy, and end with a telephone or box number. The assumption
is that the potential customer is thoroughly familiar with the product category
and needs only the basic facts to make a decision.

But big-budget broadcast and print advertising almost always deals with more
complicated and subtle sales problems and benefits. Since differences between
heavily advertised products are often slight, the way the ad illustrates or dramatizes the benefit can be as important, if not more important, than the benefit
itself. Often, the customer may not even realize he needs a given product or
service, so he must be coaxed, in indirect and offhand ways, into paying attention to the ad's message.

The three main elements of an ad are the *headline*, the *visual*, and the *copy*. Almost all ads contain all three, although some ads don't contain anything but a
picture and the company's logo. Outdoor billboards usually contain short headlines or tag lines and no copy.

The easiest way to picture how the three elements fit together is to imagine
yourself on the main floor of a department store. Suppose everyone on the main
floor is selling a competing brand of personal computer. As you walk by, each
clerk shouts something at you about the benefit his computer offers. As he
shouts, he holds up a picture of the computer, or a disk drive, or a keyboard,
or some other piece of the machine small enough for him to hold. If he can entice
you to walk over to his counter, he will start to give you his sales pitch.

What the salesman shouts at you corresponds to an ad's *headline*. What he holds
up corresponds to the ad's *visual*. His sales pitch corresponds to the ad's *copy*.

Obviously, what he shouts out to you (the headline) and holds up for you to see (the visual) constitute the main part of his "advertising." The key element in nearly every advertisement is this *headline–visual combination*. How well those two elements work to enhance each other determines how provocative the ad will be.

A good headline–visual combination has four characteristics: it is meaningful, believable, relevant, and provocative. If the consumer doesn't understand the meaning, he won't listen to the sales pitch. If he doesn't believe the basic claim, he will ignore the pitch. And if the words and the picture aren't relevant to the product's benefits, the consumer certainly won't be interested in hearing any more about it.

The word *provocative* is almost impossible to define precisely. An ad can be provocative because it is amusing, witty, beautiful, lively, informative, bold, weird, clever, startling, newsy, exciting, sexy, trendy, or classic.

## DRAMATIZING THE BENEFIT

An effective headline–visual combination does not just *state* the benefit, it *dramatizes* it. Contrary to what many advertisers think, an ad that merely illustrates the benefit does not go far enough. In order to make the benefit come alive, the ad must help consumers imagine how that benefit will improve their lives. The very essence of advertising, the core of what creative people struggle to learn how to do well, is to *dramatize the benefit*. How effectively an ad or campaign dramatizes the benefit the product or service offers the reader or viewer is what determines how provocative, and therefore how effective, that ad or campaign will ultimately be.

How do you go about dramatizing the benefit most effectively? There are as many answers to that question as there are copywriters and art directors. But there are certain guidelines you can use when you evaluate a piece of advertising. Ads that dramatize benefits well often use the headline–visual combination to *tell or begin to tell some kind of story* about the product's benefit, or the misfortune the reader will suffer if he doesn't use the product.

At bottom, advertising is *stories*. These stories usually appear to be about products and services, but what they are really about is people. Fundamentally, people have always communicated with each other with stories. All the world's great religions and political ideologies contain some formally organized system of storytelling about divine or heroic intervention in human affairs. For ordinary people, these stories bring the beliefs to life.

Great photojournalists know that the best pictures are the ones that tell the most dramatic stories. Carl Mydans, a highly celebrated photographer and correspondent for *Time* and *Life* magazines, whose career spans fifty years, is the man who took the famous picture of General Douglas MacArthur's return to the Philippines. "I am, and have always been, a storyteller," Mr. Mydans told the *New York Times* recently.

When people see the picture of General MacArthur wading to the beach, they wonder how many times did he do that . . . the general did not pose for pictures. On that occasion, I was the only still photographer in the landing craft with General MacArthur. As we went to the beach, I saw that the Seabees had gotten there ahead of us and had put out a steel pontoon ahead of the general's arrival. I jumped out ahead onto the pontoon to get a shot of the general, and suddenly the landing craft backed up and moved down the beach several hundred yards. General MacArthur did not want to land and step out on the pontoons. I never knew anybody who appreciated the value of a picture more than MacArthur.[1]

Nobody knew better than the general how important a storytelling tool the camera could be if precisely the right image could be captured, printed, and disseminated.

In *The Birth and Death of Meaning*, Ernest Becker, Pulitzer Prize–winning social theorist, wrote that all of us give our lives meaning and assert our sense of self-importance and self esteem by creating "hero-dramas" in which we live our lives as though we were actors in the drama of life. He wrote:

Role and status are a shared frame of reference that makes joint action possible; they are society's scenario for the theatrical staging of the cultural action plot . . . as in a high-school play, everyone scrambles for the lead parts. Identity is inseparable from the role one is assigned. The self-reflexive animal asks continually: "Who am I? How am I supposed to feel about myself in *this* situation? How are others supposed to feel about me?"

One of the great and lasting insights into the nature of society is that it is precisely a drama, a play, a staging. . . . The child who learns the "I" and begins to refer his action to those around him is trained *primarily as a performer*. His entire life is a training, preparation, and practice for a succession of parts in the plot—parts he can show himself worthy of filling, simply by handling them. Individuals are given parts to play in the status-role system. . . . The more intricate the staging, the more all-absorbing the play . . . if everything is split down to the finest possible point, there is less chance of chaos.

Why does man unnecessarily complicate his life? Because in this very complexity there is a challenge to ego mastery, and a denial of meaninglessness. How else would heroism be possible?[2]

In other words, dramas, or stories, come naturally to us because they are part of our very essence—the inner core of who we are and who we believe ourselves to be. (If Freud did nothing else for humanity, he demonstrated that much of our conscious behavior as adults is a dramatization of the unconscious script written for us as children.) That is why we are all fascinated by gossip, and why the inhabitants of all known societies, from the simplest to the most advanced, entertain, amuse, arouse, inspire, or anesthetize themselves primarily with theatrics of one sort or another, whether myth, novel, poem, play, opera, or TV sitcom.

It is this appetite for stories that the most effective advertising campaigns tap into. The astonishing power of television as an advertising medium lies in its capacity to tell stories about products quickly and vividly, in a kind of short-hand. Print can do precisely the same thing, albeit in a slower, more intricate, more elaborate, and less dynamic way (and, in many cases, in a more durable way).

The secret of successful advertising lies not in ever more esoteric formulas or slicker and more sophisticated research techniques, but in the ability of the agency and the advertiser to understand and take advantage of the fact that people love to hear stories about other people. The stories, and the advertising based on them, may take somewhat different forms in the future than they have in the past, but the basic elements of the mix will remain essentially the same as they have for millennia.

Notice that I wrote *"tell or begin to tell"* a story. The headline–visual combination has to tell just enough of the story to hook the reader into reading the copy. It should never tell the whole story. If the reader already knows the whole story, there's no reason to read the copy. If the benefit is stated in the headline, you've written a speech, not a play. Readers generally prefer stories about people to speeches about anything. People may listen to a speech, but they're usually willing to *pay* to see a play. A good speech can move people emotionally, change public opinion, galvanize a whole nation. It can sum up the mood of millions of people, and make those people feel gratitude or relief. But very few consumers are interested in speeches about products and their benefits. Generally you must entice or intrigue or seduce them into listening to your message—not by appealing to their sense of reason, but by plumbing the depths of their emotions.

The key question is: How do you dramatize a benefit? How do you go about making up an interesting story to tell, or begin to tell, about the benefit in your headline–visual combination? The answer is that you make use of the two essential components of drama: *conflict* and *contrast*. Charlie Chaplin once said:

Contrast spells interest: If I am being chased by a policeman, I always make the police-man seem heavy and clumsy while, by crawling through his legs, I appear light and acrobatic. If I am being treated harshly, it is always a big man who is doing it, so that, by the contrast between the big and the little, I get the sympathy of the audience, and always try to contrast my seriousness of manner with the ridiculousness of the incident.[3]

Contrast between the various physical elements in an ad or TV commercial can be used to create interest. Art directors are expert at creating and manipulating contrasting visual images—they use large type with small pictures, a large picture of a small object or a small picture of a large object, and so forth. Sometimes no picture is needed. At times, though rarely, no copy or headline is needed.

A headline–visual combination is most interesting when it leaves something to the reader's imagination. If the headline–visual combination does not require at least some work on the reader's part, or does not intrude upon his consciousness because of its obvious cleverness or striking beauty (as attractive wallpaper catches the eye because of its graceful use of form and shape or its imaginative use of colors), the ad will not engage his mind or attract his eye.

Many agencies and clients mistakenly think it is "creative" to use the visual to illustrate the literal meaning of a headline that uses an idiomatic expression, or one of the meanings of a headline that uses a double entendre. For example, they might illustrate a headline involving "the hands-on approach to banking" with a picture of a pair of hands resting comfortingly on the bank customer's shoulders. A headline about "shedding some light on" banking procedures would be illustrated by a picture of a strong light shining down on a book of procedures, or a headline including the expression "out on a limb" might be accompanied by a photograph of a man actually sitting on the limb of a tree.

Communication slows down and stalls when that sort of combination is used in an ad. Instead of the picture and the headline working synergistically to spark the reader's curiosity, the ad becomes obvious, and therefore uninteresting.

An all-copy ad with no dominant visual, or a fairly conventional picture combined with a playful headline, can work very effectively as long as the sense of playfulness is relevant to the benefit and not so arch or self-consciously cute that it overpowers the subject of the ad. Two ads of this type come to mind. One showed a car being driven hard into a turn. You could see the tires taking a set and digging in, resisting the motion of the car. The headline was "It Bites When Cornered." In a very clever way, this headline began to tell the story of the benefit the tire offered. It was provocative because it could be read two ways— that the tire had enough traction to carry a car through a tight turn at high speed (the explicit meaning), and that, like a fearsome animal, it would strike back if you challenged or threatened it. This second reading was packed with virile innuendos and macho overtones: "This is the brand for real men who earn enough to afford fast cars and are accomplished enough drivers to know how to handle them," and so forth.

Another favorite ad of mine, for the American Express Card, ran in one column in *Playbill* magazine some years ago. It listed several fancy, after-theater restaurants that honored the Card. As I remember, it was a simple ad with short copy and a line drawing of the Card. The headline read, "For Those Who Hunger After Culture." This headline is lively and provocative because it is playful and because it's a bit of a puzzle that can be read two ways. The literal, explicit way is "for those who will be hungry after the theater"; the second, "fun" way is "for those theater patrons who, in this mundane, workaday world, have a great appetite for the stimulation and excitement the art world offers cultivated people." The "story" in this case is told very quickly and in a charming way, with a simple headline that packs information, as well as a bit of fun and snob appeal, into one group of six short words.

## THE CREATIVE CONCEPT: THE BRAINS OF THE OUTFIT

Generally, the most provocative ads and commercials have what creative people call "a strong creative concept"—for short, "a concept." The concept is the executional gimmick, idea, premise, or device writers and art directors use to dramatize the benefits your product offers.

An effective creative concept does not necessarily need a great deal of concrete substance. It can have considerable symbolic significance while still appearing trivial, even silly, on the surface. Some concepts are brash and bold, others more tasteful and restrained. Neither kind is better; the best concept is the one most appropriate for the product.

Two excellent examples of concepts are the "Marlboro Man" print campaign for Marlboro cigarettes and the "Bullish On America" campaign for Merrill Lynch. The cowboy and the bull sound like the kind of simple gimmicks any high school student could dream up. But the way each of these creative concepts is executed helps provide these highly successful products with a rich chain of positive associations (a *personality*, if you will), that differentiates them from virtually identical, heavily advertised competitive products.

A striking ad for Sparkomatic car radios was headlined "How To Make Our Car Stereo As Good As a Pioneer." It showed the left half of a Sparkomatic. The right half had literally been torn off and thrown away. The idea was that a Sparkomatic had so many more features than a Pioneer that, to make it "as good as" a Pioneer, you would not have to *add* something; rather, since the Sparkomatic offered *more*, you would actually have to *tear a huge hunk of it off*. The creative concept behind this ad had to do with the visual twist inherent in showing the client's product rudely torn in half. The conventional way to illustrate the point this ad is making would be to show one Sparkomatic equaling two Pioneer radios. Here, however, the implicit violence and drama involved in tearing a high-priced piece of electronic equipment apart attracts the reader's attention. Also, since most ads for car radios show the client's product dramatically lighted and in pristine form, this ad attracts attention simply because the reader has never run across an ad for a radio that looked remotely like this one.

A recent New York City bus and subway poster campaign for *Family Circle* magazine shows young women participating in rugged outdoor pursuits like driving motorcycles or four-wheel-drive vehicles over rocks and through mountain streams. The headline is the same on all the posters: "Mama Never Said There'd Be Days Like This." This is a take-off or twist on the old phrase, "Mother always told me there'd be days like this." The original phrase referred to the kind of bad days, full of stress, tension, and turmoil, that a woman's mother had warned her about. In terms of the old phrase, mother was an authority figure, someone who knew what life was all about. The new, altered line dramatizes the idea that today's *Family Circle* reader lives the kind of fun-packed, action-filled life her mother never dreamed of, let alone told her about. Today's *Family Circle,* by implication, is not the kind of magazine an old-fashioned mother would be comfortable with. Apparently, *Family Circle* had a frumpy, stay-at-home, plain-Jane, middle-aged image that needed updating. The creative concept involved projecting a new image for the magazine by giving an old phrase a contemporary verbal and visual interpretation.

In TV, the creative concept can be subtle. The way the set is dressed, how the product is lit, the tone of the copy, the inflection in and the timbre of the announcer's voice, the melody or lyrics of a song, the personality of the celebrity on camera—all these things, which are conventionally thought of as "execution," can also be regarded as the main elements of the creative concept. An award-winning Diet Pepsi commercial consisted primarily of a tune that began with the words, "Now you see it, now you don't," accompanied by a variety of interesting close-up images of shapely women's bodies in swimsuits, close-ups of a women's lips sucking soda through a straw, product shots, and so forth. The idea was that, although you see the soda being sipped, in effect you don't "see it on you" because it doesn't contain calories that add unsightly flab. In this case, the creative concept actually consisted of executional devices and elements—an artful combination of songs and images.

It can be argued that in cases like this, the concept and the execution are one and the same. The actual substance of the creative concept or premise consists of executional methods, techniques, and devices that dramatize what you want to say in a certain way.

Grant Tinker, the guiding light behind many of TV's most famous sitcoms, has said it is not the idea but the writing and casting that is key to the success of a TV series. To some extent, the same thing is true of certain TV ad campaigns for parity products like beer, soft drinks, and hamburger chains.

The recent Michelob beer campaign is one example. The Michelob spots use a collage of quick cuts of festive, glamorous urban night scenes. The sung line, "The night belongs to Michelob," implies that the beautiful people shown whiling away their nights in Dionysian revels prefer Michelob. No specific competitive claim is made.

Some adpeople insist that campaigns like this one are inherently weak because they contain no clearly stated unique selling proposition. Such criticism misses the point. A generation raised on TV—the target audience for this spot, for the most part—watches the tube in a different, less demanding way than older people raised on radio, books, and magazines. These young people are more accepting of and more responsive to nonverbal messages than their elders. They tend to react more strongly than their parents to the total "feel," especially the visual feel, of a TV campaign, and to be more forgiving of what could be called a lack of logic in the message.

To use Marshall McLuhan's famous terms, this audience will find "cool" film, with appealing sound and pacing, where the explicit sales pitch is so oblique as to be virtually nonexistent, preferable to "hot" film, which spells out its message directly. To this young audience, the hot approach might seem too obvious, forced, wordy, and labored. It's not that they wouldn't respond in any way to a direct sales pitch; they would, if it was presented in what they perceived as a sufficiently laid-back, cool, offbeat, casual manner. But what comes most naturally to them is a visceral response to an implicit message.

Creative people who do this type of work very well are willing to spend less time showing the product close up and having the announcer reel off copy points, in order to devote more time to the slick images and production values that help enhance the spot's visceral appeal. Sophisticated ad managers understand this, too, so they go to bat with top management to get the necessary ad dollars to pay for the elaborate production values this approach demands.

My explanation may sound esoteric, but the process I'm describing is neither new nor exotic; exactly the same thing has gone on for years with print work like the Marlboro cowboy campaign, whose sales message is as indirect and visceral—and even more powerful and durable—than Michelob's.

A creative concept, then, can consist of almost anything—a performance, a statement, a picture, a way of filming, a snippet of sound or talk, a dramatic or humorous bit of stage business, a disguised sexual reference. The concept can take concrete or symbolic form in a campaign theme line, in a headline–visual combination, or in the graphics or "look" of an ad or campaign. Or it can manifest itself in what the headline or copy says, in the feeling-tone communicated by two or more people talking to each other on camera or to the audience, or in the way a celebrity is presented.

*Basically, a creative concept is an advertising idea that allows a product benefit that is either inherent or imparted to be dramatized for the consumer in a unique, compelling, provocative, memorable way.*

# IN GOOD ADVERTISING, AS IN GOOD

# MARRIAGES, WHAT YOU DON'T SAY

# OFTEN SAYS MORE THAN WHAT YOU DO SAY

## 3

If you do not understand anything else I say in this book, but you grasp what I have to tell you in the next four paragraphs, the book will have been worth its cost.

All advertising communicates in both *explicit* and *implicit* ways. An ad's explicit message is whatever the ad says directly or appears to say or show on the surface. Its explicit meaning is its first and most obvious meaning.

An ad's *implicit* messages are those that are not apparent on the surface. If the ad is poorly laid out or ugly, for example, by implication it says unattractive things about the product or service it advertises and the company paying for the advertising. If a headline is boring, or the tone of the headline is inappropriate or vulgar, it says negative things about the product and the company that produces it.

In other words, the *way* ads and commercials say what they have to say makes silent but powerful statements about the products those ads are promoting, just as the clothes we wear, the houses we live in, the accents with which we speak, and the cars we drive make statements about us. Ads have a *feeling-tone*—classy or strident, clever and warm and witty, or gross and overbearing—that has a lot to do with their ultimate success or failure. The motivational researcher Dr. Ernest Dichter put it this way:

Primitive cultures know and use nonverbal forms of human strategy without blushing. We, as logical people, insist on verbal communication, logical appeals. Our true communications, however, are not too far removed from primitive symbolism. Flags, uniforms, the way we build our homes, how we dress, and what we use and buy in everyday products are all part of a second language, a language universally spoken, hardly taught. There is much evidence to show that *it is the nonverbal implied communication that is much more often the effective one than the pure logical verbal form of communication* [emphasis added].[1]

Implicit messages that are at odds with an ad's explicit message not only fail to reinforce the message, they actually hamper the ad's effectiveness. These unconscious, nonverbal messages distract, confuse, and irritate the reader or viewer in subtle but vital ways. Try listening to a beautiful woman or a handsome man who wants to sell you something but who is missing one of his or her front teeth. Do you find yourself irritated by a person who stutters, or distracted by a salesman wearing an ill-fitting hairpiece, or by a person who speaks too loudly, too softly, or too fast? We don't want to be irritated by these superficial details because, rationally, we understand that what the person is saying is far more important than how he or she is saying it. Nevertheless, we find it hard to respect the man in the ill-fitting hairpiece. Against our will, we find ourselves questioning his judgment and wisdom. Few of us, however, will admit to being influenced by such nonrational impulses—that's why interpreting advertising research requires great skill.

An illuminating article by R. W. Apple, Jr., appeared in the *New York Times* of January 9, 1986. It described President Ronald Reagan, then at the height of his popularity, at a recent press conference. Apple writes about how Ronald Reagan, though lacking JFK's wit and Nixon's "tenacious grip on his material," dominated the press conference despite "misstatements, errors of fact and a meandering mode of presentation that would have defeated most of his recent predecessors."

Mr. Reagan, according to this article,

began his first formal news conference in almost four months with two fumbles in three sentences . . . he called the Vienna airport the Vietnam airport and called a young American killed in one attack Marsha instead of Natasha Simpson . . . Only once . . . did the President face a question that might be termed aggressive . . . [he] parried it with a joke.
     To most television viewers who saw him emerge from behind a closed door, stride purposefully down a long, imperially furnished, red-carpeted corridor, then fairly bound

onto a platform framed in the doorway of the East Room, much of the message—vigor, authority, relaxation—had been communicated before he spoke. At the same time that he capitalizes on the majesty of his office, Mr. Reagan manages to seem regular, easy, nice. . . . The White House regulars were called upon by name. . . . And at the end, Mr. Reagan managed to communicate, with a slightly baffled look and a shrug of the shoulders, that he would have been happy to keep talking with his good friends there for hours. The session may not have been the crisp, detailed articulation of American policy that some seek from a President; the text of the session, certainly, would not contain the policy nuggets with which other Presidents' news conferences were littered.

Mr. Reagan, often dubbed the Great Communicator—communicates not on an intellectual, but on an emotional level—rather like, it seems to this onlooker, a cross between Roosevelt and Eisenhower, the only two other presidents of the past half century who shared with Mr. Reagan, this deeply into their tenure, the same kind of popularity.[2]

Unfortunately, Mr. Reagan's popularity, and the public's confidence in his competence, was not to last past the Iran-Contra scandal and the stock market debacle of Black Monday, October 19th, 1987. But the point anybody who makes a living dealing with advertising and mass communication should understand is that Mr. Reagan's popularity rested not upon what he said, which was often muddled, unclear, and incorrect, but how he said it.

## ADS AS WARDROBE

How an ad looks—the type size and style, the way the headline is set, the size of the picture, the tone of the words used in the copy and headline, even the mouse type (the tiny type used to spell out required details and specifications) and its placement—all act as a sort of "wardrobe" for the company placing the ad. They give off invisible but powerful signals that tell customers whether the company is the kind with which they'd like to do business.

My favorite Ogilvy & Mather advertising is not David Ogilvy's wonderful "ticking of the clock at 60 miles an hour" ad for Rolls Royce. It is the series of ads that agency created for Mercedes Benz years ago.

At that time, ads for domestic luxury cars, all of them far better known in the United States than Mercedes Benz, featured heavily retouched color pictures of cars parked in front of mansions, surrounded by handsome people lounging about in formal dress. If you wanted to let people know you were selling a fancy car, advertisers reasoned, you showed it parked in a fancy place and draped with fancy people. Ogilvy's efforts, on the other hand, were full-page, black-and-white newspaper ads that looked almost like editorials. Cars, at least

Mercedes Benz cars, they seemed to say, are *serious business*. These ads were clearly written not just to be looked at, but to be read.

The copy, written in Ogilvy's typically gentlemanly, upper-crust way, was packed with explicit information about the technical sophistication and inherent superiority of Mercedes Benz cars. The Ogilvy people knew that buyers of expensive cars would be willing to read extensive copy about a high-ticket item. They also knew that the mere fact that there were enough technically outstanding features to fill one newspaper page after another with copy would, in itself, impress consumers. The consumer would think, in effect, "They wouldn't dare write so much about the machine if it weren't true, and nobody in his right mind would take up so much space and spend so much money and use so many words if it weren't important." The single impression that was conveyed, not only by what the ads stated explicitly but by the way they chose to state it, was one of *quality*. In this case, the implicit message not only reinforced the explicit message, but was probably even more powerful because it affected the much broader audience who noticed but did not read the ads.

In implicit ways, ads either invite the reader or viewer to participate and get involved with what they're saying and the way they say it, or they don't. Cluttered layouts and verbose copy containing disparate elements are like a poorly groomed, long-winded salesman who is indifferent to the value of his prospect's time.

Much of what a client pays an agency for is its intuitive ability to meld complementary implicit and explicit messages in an ad, so as to leave a single powerful, positive impression with the reader or viewer. That's why, when an art director uses a certain style of type and makes the logo a given size, and the client insists the logo be made more prominent—as many do, because they think more people will notice it—the client is making a potentially serious mistake.

Art directors and writers study ads and commercials constantly. Something inside their heads is tuned into the particular layouts and video techniques that are current—which of these is likely to be a passing fad, which are merely trendy and may have value for a short while, and which are classic. When these people create advertising, they use this finely developed aesthetic sense. In a sense, each ad or commercial your agency creates is a house of cards. Each element in each piece of advertising is conceived in a way that makes it an organic part of a coherent whole that is quite fragile, because it is based on gut feeling and aesthetic judgment. When a client starts reshuffling the pieces, the entire structure is in danger of collapse.

In most cases, the best thing clients can do with the advertising that is presented to them by their agency is to make sure it is on strategy and then leave it alone. What may seem like small, day-to-day adjustments and accommodations in layouts or copy, involving apparently minor aesthetic matters, can seriously weaken an ad's positive implicit message.

Mies van der Rohe wrote "God is in the details." He was referring to architecture, but he could just as well have been referring to the architecture of your advertising.


## A BIT MORE ABOUT ADS BEING MORE LIKE PLAYS THAN SPEECHES

Speeches are primarily intellectual events with emotional overtones, whose prime purpose is to get people to think. But to be effective, speechmakers must be aware of the implicit messages their presence and manner of speaking send to the audience. In that sense, speeches can bear some resemblance to ads. Plays, however, bear a much greater resemblance to advertising, because plays dramatize a point of view and are primarily emotional events with intellectual overtones.

A playwright may or may not be interested in advancing a point of view, but unless he can get his audience to react emotionally, whatever his motives, his play will fail. A speechmaker approaches the podium in a relatively undramatic manner. The audience waits to hear what he will say so they can begin thinking about it. But when the curtain rises on the first act of a play, the stage set immediately begins to "talk" to the audience, in a silent but powerful way, about the nature of the play and the concerns of the playwright. When a reader turns the page in a magazine, or when your TV commercial begins, it is as though the curtain is going up on a little playlet your agency has created. Just as everything on stage must have something to do with the nature of the play, so everything in your print ad or TV commercial must bear directly upon the explicit and implicit messages you wish to send.

The attitude many advertisers have is, "Yeah, sure, I understand that a noisy restaurant or a snotty waiter can ruin a good meal even though they don't affect the actual taste of my food. But when it comes to advertising, I've got to get my message across in a big, bold brassy way, because people have other things to do than read or watch my advertising."

My point is not that *all* advertising must be restrained, excessively dignified, or "tasteful" to the point of torpor. Splashy, spirited, brash approaches often work wonders. My point is this: If you understand and appreciate the difference between implicit and explicit messages, and the importance of the implicit ones, you will be in the best position to help your agency create effective advertising for your company.

# SURPRISE!

# 4

Q: If there was one thing you'd like to tell advertisers, one mistake many of them make that they shouldn't make, what would it be?

A: It's the mistake of walking away from advertising that makes them nervous. Because great work should make them nervous. It's the mistake of walking away from anything that isn't all too comfortable and all too familiar. It shouldn't be comfortable. It should make them squirm a little, startle them a little, keep them awake a few nights wondering, "Should I or should I not run that?" That's the kind of work they shouldn't turn their back on. Too many clients do.

—Philip B. Dusenberry, chairman and chief creative officer, BBDO Worldwide

Whenever possible, the headline–visual combination in an ad, or the premise or the concept of a TV spot, should contain an *element of surprise,* a quality of the unexpected. In other words, the choice of words and pictures you use to dramatize your benefit, or to introduce your product or service, should contain something new, something the reader or viewer wouldn't ordinarily expect to see. The newness should be based upon the benefit the product offers, but it doesn't have to come out of the product; it can come out of your choice of words, or the way the words relate to the picture. It can come from a new way of using photography or illustrations. For example, if all your competitors are using campaigns with a high-tech look, maybe it's time for you to use illustrations. If everybody else is using long copy, maybe you can use short copy to good advantage, or vice versa. I realize that for most large clients, this is easier said than done. There's something comforting about having your advertising look a lot like your competitors' advertising. But the last thing fresh, compelling advertising ever looks like is everybody else's advertising.

## WHEN YOU EVALUATE ADVERTISING, PREPARE TO BE ASTONISHED

An advertising agency that shows you work that does not contain some sense of the unexpected—at least a few surprises—is simply not doing its job the way it should. I am quite serious when I say that one of the main responsibilities any advertising agency has is to prepare, propose, and fight for ads that make clients nervous. Furthermore, they should keep clients nervous over the years by showing them exciting, unexpected ways of saying what they have to say. As Roy Grace, quoting the legendary Bill Bernbach, told an *Ad Age* reporter:

Bernbach used to say, "Make them nervous. Our job is to make them nervous, to give the client what we think they need, not what they want. No one likes to be made nervous. Everyone likes to be comfortable, but no one really likes comfortable advertising." So my job is to make sure the client is a little nervous.[1]

What "advertising's hottest creative director," Tom McElligott of Fallon McElligott in Minneapolis, said in the July 1986 issue of *Inc.* magazine is appropriate:

. . . the bigger problem stems from a kind of misrepresentation about how effective most advertising really is. And most of it—I'm talking here of somewhere between 95 and 98% of it—just doesn't work. It doesn't break through, it doesn't get by all the other advertising clutter. That happens for a couple of reasons. Either the ads are strategically stupid, or they are executed stupidly, or both. And the reason for it—once you get past the small advertisers, the little retailers who simply don't know any better and haven't got a marketing guy on board or an agency—has to do with agencies playing it safe, going with the known quantity, the formula-type ad. In order to protect the account, they shy away from giving clients the sort of advertising that makes the palms sweat a little, that makes you a bit nervous. In my opinion, at least, these are the only ads worth running.
    **Inc:** Are there any rules for developing the type of ads that break through?
    The rule, pretty much, is to break the rules. If you break the rules, you're going to stand a better chance of breaking through the clutter than if you don't. If you try to live with the rules, in all likelihood the work will be derivative, it won't be fresh, it won't have the necessary ingredients to disarm the consumer, who increasingly has got his defenses up against all sorts of advertising messages coming his way.[2]

# NEWS IS ALMOST ALWAYS A SURPRISE, BUT

# NEWS IS NOT ENOUGH

## 5

In the past forty years, U.S. consumers have changed more than any group of people of similar size in history. As late as the early 1950s, few Americans had traveled very much or very far. TV was in its infancy. Young people who married were prepared to do things pretty much the way their parents had done them. The advertising audience was relatively passive; they read ads to learn about new products and were willing to try them "if," as my grandmother used to say, "the advertisements speak well of them."

News and entertainment are much cheaper and more accessible commodities today than most people ever dreamed they'd be at the end of World War II. And the line between news and entertainment—in big-time sports; on the local and network TV news; on the morning shows and feature programs like "20/20" and "60 Minutes"; and in so-called news magazines like *People, Sports Illustrated, Newsweek,* and *Time*—has dimmed considerably, if not disappeared. News about products is no longer enough to attract audiences' attention; the news advertising brings to their homes must be combined with entertainment in a far more imaginative way than it was, say, ten years ago.

By "imaginative" I don't mean the extensive use of whiz-bang, trendy, boffo, rock-'em-sock-'em, hard rock techniques that may appeal superficially and temporarily to young people. I mean better graphics and a wittier, more sophisticated choice of words in print and TV copy than many clients are used to.

These changes in mass communication and audience expectations pose a serious problem to all advertisers, because the task of keeping up with them, let alone learning how to use them to commercial advantage, can be a full-time job. But they're especially vexing to the individuals who run most major corporations. For the most part, these are men in their late fifties or early sixties who, for a generation, have devoted most of their best waking hours to their jobs and companies. They spend their working lives in offices and boardrooms, on golf courses, in airplanes, and at sales conventions. To an increasing extent, they're out of the country on business. There are not enough hours in the day for them to keep up with everything management consultants and business school textbooks tell them they ought to be familiar with.

It goes without saying that these executives find themselves somewhat out of touch with the mass of consumers their advertising is trying to reach. Often the only advertising these people have time to pay close attention to and know much about is the advertising published and broadcast by companies within their own industry. In my experience. the result is that the ad executions many of these executives tend to favor are similar in style and tone to the appeals they themselves responded to, or saw other people respond to, thirty years ago, when they were in college or just starting their business careers. More often than not, contemporary audiences find these executions dated, obvious, and dull.

I don't mean to imply that in order to produce contemporary advertising every board chairman and president must be on intimate terms with every Tom, Dick, and Harriet in the United States. But the ultimate responsibility for effective advertising rests squarely on the shoulders of the people at the top of the pyramid. So it is incumbent on top decision makers to keep the lines of communication open between themselves and the people who *are* in touch with contemporary tastes—their ad managers and ad agencies. The more frequently, intimately, and openly the head honchos deal with these groups, and the more confidence they have in them, the less isolated their companies will be from the consumers they're trying to reach, and the more effective their advertising is likely to be.

All this may seem like simple common sense to the savvy ad managers and agency people who work for and with sophisticated advertisers. But most advertisers are not sophisticated. Nearly twenty-five years of dealing with major advertisers has convinced me that the practice of maintaining a close working relationship with their advertising people and agencies is a lot less common among company chairmen and presidents than it should be.

George Bernard Shaw said, "Progress is impossible without change; and those who cannot change their minds cannot change anything." It should not be too much to ask that those people who run the major American corporations, and who keep their ad agencies and ad managers at arm's length, become more knowledgeable about the advertising process and more intimately involved with their advertising agencies.

One man who has changed the way his company deals with his agencies is Reuben Mark, chairman–CEO of Colgate-Palmolive Company. According to *Ad Age* (April 20, 1987):

. . . those who know him assert that his leadership has been critical in transforming Colgate into a place where employees and their work are highly valued. The employees, in turn, have produced financial results that are breaking corporate records . . . It became evident last year that Colgate's plan to distinguish itself as a leader in creativity was a continuing commitment . . . with the hiring of Clay Timon—whose entire career had been on the agency side—as the company's first worldwide advertising director, Mr. Mark set in motion a strategy to get more mileage out of Colgate's ad dollars.

One after another, the company's ad campaigns have received critical acclaim: one after another, those involved at Colgate or its agencies pointed to Mr. Mark.

Mr. Mark's role in the actual advertising decisions is limited . . . "I have considerable involvement in agency relationships and problem-solving," [he said]. "On a regular basis, it consists of discussions . . . with the top management of the agency . . . identifying the problem areas, the opportunities."

Every four or five months he has breakfast with 10 to 15 creative and account staffers from the agencies, without the "big bosses" on hand, to learn what's going on in the trenches.

On getting together with the lower-level people at the agencies he said, "The biggest aspect is not the hard stuff of what comes out. It's that I get to talk to these people and take their temperatures, see what the problems are and show that I am genuinely interested in what they're doing."

Mr. Mark has even enrolled all agency people working on Colgate's business in the company's employee stock-benefit plan. And he meets with this special group of shareholders periodically to report on how "their" company is doing. At the annual partnership meetings, Colgate management listens to the agencies' evaluation of whether Colgate is living up to its promises. Are Colgate's executives streamlining their approval process? Is the business profitable for the agency?

A further example of Colgate fulfilling its partnership pledge: Mr. Mark disclosed that both Y&R and FCB, at the start of their relationships, underestimated the cost of doing business with Colgate . . . So, last year, their commissions were raised to the standard 15%, up from a slightly lower percentage that Colgate historically had paid.

Mr. Mark himself admitted that the whole process—such as talking about agencies as partners—sounds cliched and not very profound. "You're successful if we're successful." "Think entrepreneurial—what would you do if it was your business?" "Put yourself in the consumers' shoes."

"You've heard it all before," he commented. "It sounds very trite." But it becomes real when carried out.

As involved as Mr. Mark is in the push for creative excellence, he keeps his hands off the actual advertising's creative approach.

"That would be misplaced because if every piece of copy has to go through me, then I'm emasculating everybody down the line," he said.

"It's the most unusual situation I have ever seen in all my experience with clients," said Charles Taney, the FCB exec VP who heads the Colgate business.[1]

Here are Reuben Mark's ten commandments for creative excellence, as listed in *Ad Age*:

Be the best client they have.

We must really care.

True partnership/mutual trust.

Ask for excellence.

Clear, honest direction.

Look for the big idea.

Streamline approval procedure.

Personal involvement of top management of client/agency.

Ensure agency profitability.

Be human.

The chairman of every corporation with an ad budget would do well to make these ten commandments his guide for dealing with his ad agencies.

IF ECCLESIASTES COULD KEEP IT SIMPLE, AND

ABE LINCOLN AND CARL SANDBURG AND WALT

DISNEY AND E. B. WHITE AND ERNEST HEMINGWAY

AND CHARLES SCHULTZ AND WALT KELLY

AND GIACOMETTI AND MIES VAN DER ROHE

AND HENRY MOORE COULD KEEP IT SIMPLE,

WHY MUST YOU AND YOUR COHORTS DRIVE YOUR

AGENCY CRAZY BY MAKING IT COMPLICATED?

# 6

I said earlier that some of the most provocative ads are those that require a little work on the reader's part. The key phrase is "a little." An ad whose creative concept is complicated, cumbersome, or too elaborate will strike the reader or viewer as obscure, and he will pass it by if he's reading or ignore it if he's watching TV.

Ads must not only be simple conceptually, like religious parables, they must also have the *appearance* of being simple and easily grasped. That is, the layout and graphic treatment of the ad should make it look inviting to read rather than cluttered or complicated. An ad may contain many visual elements, perhaps half a dozen or even a dozen pictures or more. But the way those pictures are combined with the headline and copy, and the way everything is arranged on the page, must strike the reader as clear, logical, and simple. If the reader's eye must wander all over the page trying to help his brain figure out what the ad is about, the ad is bound to fail.

Print ads should have strong, simple, concise layouts and headlines. Whether the copy is long or short, it should not look dense and hard to read, and it should make one point and one point only. TV commercials also must make only one point. The campaign they're a part of, too, must be single-minded. No matter how many commercials your campaign includes, they should all make the same point, a point that can be summed up in no more than a dozen words, over and over again.

It's natural for clients, who are fascinated with their own products and proud of the efforts of the employees who have conceived those products, to want to boast about every last one of a product's benefits. *This impulse must be resisted.* Making an ad or commercial try to say more than one simple thing at a time is like inviting two people to give a lost driver directions at the same time.

If you have more than one thing to say in an ad, rethink the problem. If there is absolutely no way to simplify your message, make one message paramount and the second message subordinate—*clearly* subordinate, both visually and verbally. If there is absolutely no way to do that, allow your agency enough creative freedom to work with one dominant visual and a headline that alludes to your double message.

It has always amazed me how often clients, especially inexperienced clients, insist on stuffing everything they can think of into every ad they run. Their "logic" is, "I've damn well paid for all that space, and I'm going to use all of it." But using white space properly in your ad can help to isolate it from editorial matter and the other ads on the page, and draw the reader's attention to it.

Corporations are run by committees. All too often, each committee member feels compelled to add his favorite little bit to the advertising he's being asked to approve. As the ads travel up the corporate ladder, the process continues, until the advertising that's finally approved bears little resemblance to what was originally offered. In almost every case, the advertising winds up more complicated, less focused, and dull.

The smaller your ad is, and the shorter your TV commercial, the more important it is that its message be focused.

Ads with many pictures can work quite well, depending, of course, on the point you're trying to illustrate. But as a general rule, one picture and one headline work far better than one headline and many pictures or, worse, several headlines, or a headline and several subheads combined with one or more pictures.

The ads that top writers and art directors admire most, as shown year after year among the winners and finalists in the important award shows in New York, almost always have one picture with one headline and a simple copy block.

It would be instructive for clients to spend a few days every year looking at the portfolios of the world's top advertising photographers, as agency art directors do on a regular basis. In almost every photograph, the eye is drawn toward one central point. That point can be anywhere in the picture, but there is never more than a single one. If there are two objects in the picture, one is always there to highlight the other. If there are two objects in a shot—for example, two beautifully lit, perfect cultured pearls—they are framed and composed so that the two make up a single unit; if not, one will be used to define and dramatize the other.

There are ways to use multiple photographs or illustrations in an ad without making the ad seem busy and crowded. The key is to make sure there are no disparate elements in the ad. If the concept or premise of the ad, the single point it's trying to get across, embraces and unites all of the elements, you can use literally hundreds of pictures and still wind up with a provocative ad.

Some years ago, I wrote a two-page ad for Volvo whose main element was an illustrated, stylized color map of the United States. There were a dozen different drawings of Volvos on the map, along with a number of illustrations of famous vacation spots. The headline read, "The Volvo Guide To The Worst Vacation Spots In America." The copy block set close to each Volvo explained how one or another Volvo attribute helped the people in the car deal with the unique difficulties they encountered when vacationing in that particular location. The whimsical tone of the headline made the ad inviting to read. The copy and the illustrations all shared that tone. The single point the ad made was that Volvo was a tough, well-made car. Nobody could call the ad simple, but I don't believe anybody who knew anything about advertising would call it complicated, either; as with the Mercedes Benz ads I mentioned earlier, every element in it was part of a common theme and helped advance the same simple premise.

# WARNING: ADVERTISING RESEARCH CAN BE HARMFUL TO YOUR HEAD

## 7

At the annual meeting of the [the name of the huge New York City conglomerate-type agency and its chairman are omitted], chairman and chief executive, disclosed that the holding company and its agencies are in the midst of developing proprietary research that will be used in making advertising.

. . . it will not be based on historical data but rather, "in prognostication of the future behavioral needs of the consumer." It should be in use by next year, he said.

—*New York Times*, May 20, 1987

Perhaps no other agency service is as abused and misused as the research department.

Often, in new business presentations, agency management insists the role of the researcher is to "sell the agency." That means the researcher must come up with some technique or system that sounds proprietary in order to convince prospective clients that he has access to insights other agencies don't have.

Research is research. There are expert researchers and inexpert researchers, of course, and sloppy, careless researchers and meticulous, painstaking researchers. But the key to successful research lies not in a magic formula connoted by yet another new set of initials with a high-tech sound, but in how the agency uses the research and how well the individual researchers within the agency relate to the individuals in the creative, media, and account service departments.

Once an agency gets an account, some management supervisors urge the research department to "move things along." That's a euphemism for "hurry up and give the client some convincing numbers, so he can make a decision, we can place some advertising, and the agency can make its commission."

Some creative people are too defensive about research results, or ignore research entirely, because they feel the dictates of the researchers, as interpreted by the agency's account service department or by the client, will hamper their imagination and thwart their creative impulses.

Another downside area, according to research consultant Murray Hysen, is that some brand or ad managers have short-term orientations that emphasize "*big* winners." "What's more, he adds, "They want them *immediately*, because they want to use these 'successes' as stepping stones to other, more important jobs, and they want to show their superiors they are capable of doing super-well, super-quickly."

In the worst circumstances, these pressures tend to force research into a role it cannot hope to fulfill—predicting big winners. Hysen, who served as research director of Wells, Rich Greene for seventeen years and now consults for several agencies and clients, says: "There is no person, there is no system that can predict copy test results. The proper use of this type of research is as an aid to judgment in the development and evaluation of advertising."

Life is untidy, and people's thought processes are messy and contradictory. To the degree that research is an accurate reflection of the way people think and feel, it, too, will be imprecise, a bit baffling at times, and often inconclusive. In the worst case—and unfortunately there are many worst cases—Murray Hysen says:

Common sense goes out the window. For example, people forget that the emotional component in advertising is very hard to measure in any research. All too often, people wind up interpreting numbers slavishly, totally ignoring the limitations of what copy research can and cannot deliver . . .
   Actually there are four basic phases of research involvement. The first stage relates to planning, and the emphasis here is on learning and understanding as much as we can about the market, the product, and the consumer. At this point we usually rely on data from large, scientifically drawn samples. The second phase is small-scale qualitative copy research. It is diagnostic in nature and is designed to provide guidance as advertising is being developed. The third step is formal, quantitative copy testing, usually based on

either in-home or in-theater exposure and relying on either twenty-four-hour or seventy-two-hour recall data or predisposition scores as the basis for deciding whether or not the campaign should be run. The final stage involves tracking studies, measuring changes in awareness, attitudes and behavior as the campaign is run. It is in the second and third stages where most of the abuses occur.

Most quantitative copy testing systems are very good at delivering clear winners and clear losers. It is in the middle, where the vast majority of the ads and commercials fall, that the danger lies. Numbers are frequently stretched and twisted out of shape in order to conform with the prejudices of one or another ad agency or client power group.

Certain successful pieces of advertising need time to seat themselves in the public consciousness. Top creative people insist that in many cases, the more imaginative a commercial is, the less likely it is to achieve a high recall score after only one exposure. Their view, which I share, is that many viewers will ignore or misunderstand commercials that are different from most others, the first time around. Some part of the viewer's brain, however, does take note of an approach that seems fresh and interesting; his curiosity piqued, he is on the lookout for that commercial from then on. The second, third, or fourth time he sees it he will pay more attention in order to see exactly what this strange new bird is all about. If he likes what he sees, not only will he pay attention to what the jingle or theme line says, he will tend to remember copy points. He may even tell his friends about it. David Letterman may joke about it in his monologue. By that time, the product, the slogan, and the campaign are on the way to becoming famous.

The best research people fight hard every day to resist any pressures. They try not to oversell what they have to offer or to misinterpret the precision with which they can measure advertising or audience reaction. They struggle to maintain an informal, nonthreatening, mutually supportive relationship with creative and account people. Murray Hysen insists, quite correctly, that "The purpose of research is not to provide all answers, but rather to provide meaningful information and to help guide the exercise of the kind of good judgment, intuition, and plain common sense that all successful advertising is based on." He adds a word of warning: "People should accept the fact that research can tell about what *has* happened better than it can predict what *will* happen."

The main problem for the ad manager who relies excessively on high twenty-four-hour recall scores or preference changes is that his perspective can easily deteriorate into a desperate search for creative executions that follow a formula or fit precisely into one or two rigid, preconceived patterns. That kind of mind set invariably demoralizes agency creative departments. Knowing the score, as it were, they lapse into giving the client the only thing they know he will buy—frequently an on-camera announcer talking directly to the camera and pointing to the product, or two women in a kitchen or laundry room raving about some mundane household product or food that works so well or tastes so good, it has virtually changed their lives.

## THE BLUEPRINT SHOULDN'T SHOW IN THE FINISHED HOUSE

Brand managers often insist that characters in commercials mouth the half dozen copy points that "research" has shown segments of the audience may, just may, be capable of remembering. Too often, the exact words of the marketing strategy, stilted as they sound, find their way into the mouths of the characters in a commercial. Or one character may repeat the main copy point several times in thirty seconds because "research" has suggested that repetition helps recall.

In these cases, the research "tail" is wagging the dog. I don't believe these types of commercials, no matter how high their copy test scores, do as good a job of selling as commercials using characters who sound more natural because they speak like real human beings instead of robots.

I firmly believe advertising should not only sell a product or service, but that, whenever possible (and I think it is always possible), the way the print ad or commercial is executed should leave a positive impression about the product and the advertiser in the minds of the viewing and reading public. When the first piece of advertising fails to establish the basis for an eventual sale *and* make a friend of the reader or viewer, it makes things more difficult for the second, third, and fourth pieces of advertising.

The argument is often made that it is simply not logical to run commercials with less than the highest recall scores, because the more people who recall the commercial, and the more copy points that are played back in the research, the more effective the commercial is likely to be. I know of no proof that that is so. I have never seen indisputable scientific proof that higher recall scores correlate directly with higher sales. There are simply too many variables between the test and the sale. I do know that people who don't talk like people when they try to sell me things, and people who repeat sales messages two and three times in thirty seconds, and people who try to sell me things at the rate of seventy-seven or eighty words in thirty seconds, irritate me. They make me feel my intelligence is being underestimated. And I firmly believe that the mass of the viewing audience is as intelligent as I am and has more or less the same sensibilities.

# LET'S NOT BE QUITE SO LITERAL

## 8

Mr. Stanfill is "the kind of talent we need here," Mr. Hawley says. "We can always buy creative talent." "You're wrong, Phil," Mr. Gold retorts. "You think creative talent can be bought as a commodity. You see guys like Eisner as a little crazy or a little off the wall. . . . Every great studio in this business has been run by crazies. What do you think Walt Disney was? The guy was off the . . . goddamned wall. [The Company] is a creative institution. . . . What's been wrong with this institution over the past twenty years is that it hasn't been run by crazies . . . Clean out your image of crazies. We're talking about creative crazies. . . . We can always buy M.B.A. talent" [like Mr. Stanfill].

. . . Mr. Bass, who has always described himself as a hard-asset man, uncomfortable with the ephemeral products of Hollywood, nevertheless shows unique insight into how to succeed in show business. He discerns the superficiality of the creative-versus-business argument and recognizes that creative flair and business discipline are both essential for durable success in entertainment.

—David McClintick, Review of *Storming the Magic Kingdom: Wall Street, the Raiders, and the Battle for Disney,* by John Taylor, *New York Times Book Review,* May 10, 1987, p. 1

*The time*: 11:30 P.M.

*The place*: The lounge of the New York Hilton.

*The people*: Two clients, one older, one quite young; a junior and a senior account woman from the ad agency; and me. The older of the two clients has white hair. The young one has no hair, but he has an MBA from Amos Tuck. Clearly, he is one of those hard-asset types.

*The problem*: The client's prestigious business magazine is losing market share to its main competitor because young businesspeople think his magazine is stuffy, pompous, and dull and his competitor's is brash, vigorous, and lively.

*The solution*: A ninety-second direct-response TV commercial with an 800 number, to sell six-month subscriptions. It has to be cheap to shoot; it should have a tone appropriate to the magazine's image; and it has to mention loads of cut prices, free offers, and a terrific subscription premium at least two and preferably three times. Most important, it must appeal strongly to the affluent young businesspeople who tend to favor the other guy's magazine.

*Our solution*: A cute, slightly wacky, but charming receptionist, facing the camera, talks to an off-camera magazine salesman who wants to sell the owner of the giant corporation for whom she works a subscription to the client's magazine. She is skeptical and will not let him through until he gives her his whole sales pitch. Her presence adds whimsy and sex appeal to the commercial, which will help it appeal to ambitious young businesspeople. Since we can use a one-wall set, the spot will be cheap to shoot, but, in keeping with the magazine's image, it will have an upscale look. And if the actress is directed properly, the whimsical tone of the commercial will help loosen up the magazine's stuffy image. The mass of detail about the subscription will come from the off-camera salesman, so the audience will hear lots of hard-sell copy, but it will be easier to take because the viewers can watch the actress's reactions.

The older client likes the spot and wants to go with it, but this is not his show. The younger man doesn't like it. Or, better put, whether or not he likes it is irrelevant, because he is afraid of it. Why? "We don't have magazine salesmen selling our magazine. People will think we sell our magazines door to door. We don't do that." Looking at his older companion, he adds for emphasis, "We've never done that." He is very polite. He smiles. He allows as how the commercial is very "zingy." He fingers his rep tie. "Can you imagine The Founder ever doing that?" he asks the older man rhetorically.

The older man knew the founder. He shakes his head no. The Founder, he reminds us offhandedly, has been dead oh, say fifteen, eighteen years. Clearly, he was in his dotage before anybody every heard of 800 numbers. His point, apparently, which is lost on his young companion, is that it is unwise to base today's decisions on what one thinks The Founder would have done twenty years ago. The young man shakes his head sadly, apologetically. "He'd turn over in his grave."

The senior account woman is tired, but game. She takes a deep breath. "But the approach is obviously whimsical," she says. "Our audience is highly affluent and college-educated. Do you think they will take the spot so literally? Won't they realize this is just a device to sell subscriptions?"

"We're not the type of magazine that's sold door to door. This is tantamount to misrepresentation." The young client frowns, chuckles, looks sad. "We could be sued."

The account woman protests that although we'd had an imposing number of requirements, we had managed to satisfy every single one. "This," she says, "was not an easy assignment. You have to allow for some creative license here. I mean, we don't want some Crazy Eddie–type pitchman yelling at the audience about what a terrific deal this is on a magazine that's virtually the Bible of the grey, pin-striped suit set." Her voice rises a bit. "We've figured out a clever way to get across all this hard-sell information about a prestige product in 90 seconds . . . the tongue-in-cheek quality of the spot helps our target audience under-stand, by implication, that we're not the stuffy tome they think we are. I hope you realize this spot sells several different ways, on a couple of different levels. Frankly, I think it's quite an achievement, creatively speaking."

Lamely, the junior account woman suggests we super *magazine not sold door-to-door* in small type under the telephone number. It's not a great idea, but it's not a bad idea either. Nobody but the client would read it, of course, but it might get us past our present impasse. No dice. The client is not buying.

*The moral*: When they are clients, even magazine publishers, who should know better, are inclined to take every piece of their own advertising literally. They honestly believe consumers are unable to make the leap of imagination neces-sary to understand the difference between actors and TV commercials on the one hand and the actual product or service on the other.

A surprising number of clients, especially those who've never had any interest or experience in anything like amateur theatricals or writing scripts for school plays, lack a gut feel for the way consumers respond to the written or spoken word. These clients are whizzes with those parts of advertising that involve numbers, but when it comes to combining words and pictures to tell stories, they lack the feel of the clay in their fingers. When they evaluate advertising executions, they project their own failing onto the mass audience. They do not understand that consumers react to ads in a generalized, unanalytical, emotional way—the way most people react to most things.

Consumers are much more imaginative than many advertisers—especially some numbers-happy M.B.A.'s—are willing to give them credit for. Readers and viewers do not have to be led by the hand to understand what a client's advertising is getting at. All they need is a couple of key verbal and visual guideposts; they are quite capable of filling in the blanks.


## THE YUPPIES IN THE PENTHOUSE

Many advertisers favor the condescendingly explicit approach I call the "yuppies in the penthouse" method of advertising. If they are advertising a whiskey, for example, in order to show that their whiskey is the favorite of young successful, upwardly mobile people, they literally show these people in tuxedos drinking the specified brand at a cocktail party in a penthouse high above a glamorous city—with a vague, wooden headline that says something like, "When you've got it made, this is the drink that makes the party," or ". . . to life!" or "Success comes in many forms."

An example of the opposite approach is the daring and award-winning Chivas Regal Scotch campaign (see Chapter 16 for examples), which built the brand. These ads never say anything literal about smoothness or good taste; they don't show others that you're "making it" by buying Chivas. The campaign conveys the message that Chivas is a classy, quality Scotch entirely through the visual and verbal cues in the ads. Most of the ads contain a big picture of the bottle and a headline that refers to situations or relationships between people that have some relevance to the drinking or buying of fine Scotch, or to the reward for good service or the loving care a gift of fine Scotch symbolizes. Symbolically, and often in a tongue-in-cheek manner, the ads tell stories about people, in which Scotch is involved in some emotionally significant way.

These ads communicate quality in a powerful way, but largely by implication. Without giving it a great deal of conscious thought, the audience assumes Chivas Regal is a sophisticated whiskey, drunk by sophisticated people, because the ads tell their story in a sophisticated way.

Executions that use words and pictures that supply the reader with carefully selected, evocative cues that encourage him to tell his own story, or to finish telling the one the words and pictures start, are very effective. The more literal approach, in which the headline and the visual pretty much tell the reader the entire story, is one that treats the reader as a spectator; Chivas Regal's approach invites him to become a participant.

When it began, Marlboro cigarette advertising did use copy ("Come to where the flavor is/Come to Marlboro country"). But for many years, they have maintained the cigarette's macho personality without using any copy at all—except, of course, for the mandatory surgeon general's warning. This campaign doesn't literally *say* anything about the product to anybody. By implication, it invites the reader to identify himself with the cowboy, and the cowboy with the cigarette.

The handsome Absolut vodka campaign (see examples in Chapter 16) implies good taste and contemporaneousness without using any of those words—without even showing the bottle in a social situation. The cues in these ads are subtle and powerful. They have to do with the way the bottle is lit and shot, the selection of props, and the puns and word plays in the headlines. Some of the ads become a kind of one- or two-second literary game that a sophisticated audience might be inclined to play. A highly imaginative ad for Absolut in the May 18, 1987, issue of *New York* magazine featured a stark, blank white page of very heavy paper. The entire ad was embossed. Most of the page was occupied by a raised impression of the Absolut vodka bottle within a circle. The bold headline embossed on the bottom read "ABSOLUT IMPRESSION."

The affluent, sophisticated young drinker is attracted to these ads because of the way they look as much as by what they say. Having played its word/picture game, as it were, the reader has become somewhat familiar with the product. He feels closer to it than he would have if the ad were more literal. He has begun to feel it might be his kind of alcohol—the kind that would fit into his metier and mark him as a person who knows his vodkas.

You may well ask why, if this approach is more effective, so many advertisers stick with less memorable, more literal approaches. The answer, as I have indicated, is that the overwhelming majority of ad managers and their bosses react to advertising literally. They simply do not understand that more subtle advertising can work harder.

Another problem is that the Chivas Regal/Absolut Vodka type of advertising is very hard to learn how to do. Perhaps no more than 25 percent of the people who can create advertising can do it well. It's much easier, and quicker, to attempt to convey a pricey image for whiskey, for instance, by using the yuppies in the penthouse approach. Since obvious, literal solutions to creative problems are what most clients buy and all that most agencies are capable of doing well, those are the kinds of ads that fill our magazines.

It is not that more obvious executions don't work at all. When they're very well done, they can work quite well. It's simply that more subtle, less literal executions of advertising strategies work better, in part because they appeal to consumers on a deeper, more complex level and in part because they stand out sharply from a plethora of more conventional, literal approaches.

There are two kinds of effective ad managers: those who have innate creative flair and those who don't, but who have the courage to risk trying an advertising execution with which they are not completely comfortable.

Most ad managers use literal interpretations to evaluate creative work because these kinds of interpretations seem most "logical" or "reasonable." But these are usually rationalizations. Literal interpretations are basically defensive in nature; psychologically, they protect timid individuals from ways of thinking that involve breaking "logical," intellectualized boundaries.

# TO ARMS! TO ARMS! EVERY MAN LOOK SHARP!

# THE DAMN AGENCY IS ASKING US TO TRUST

# ITS *INTUITION* AGAIN!

## 9

"It's good because I say it's good."

When all is said and done, you place your advertising with a particular agency because you have faith in their judgment when they tell you that the advertising they create for you will work. Chances are you will never have definitive proof that it worked. Even if you did, it would be after the fact. What's more, if it did work, you'd never know whether different creative work, created by a different agency, would have worked even better.

How does the agency know the advertising they create for you will work? They don't. They think it will—on the basis of their experience with advertising they've created for other clients. Since some of the advertising they have created earlier has failed to work, what it comes down to is that you're buying the new shop the way you buy most things—on faith.

Anybody can claim anything he wants to in the advertising business because there's no sure way to prove very much of anything. There's nothing unusual about that. Lots of businesses—psychiatry, architecture, politics, the movie business, the fashion business, the publishing business, and the investment business, to name just a few—work the same way.

But clients are not comfortable with this situation. Clients fancy themselves hardheaded businessmen. So they listen carefully to all the new business pitches. They pay attention to all the stuff about research and media and strategic analysis and the agency's long history of successes with similar products. They visit each agency and walk through its halls. They talk to friends whose companies are with other agencies. They weigh all the evidence. In the end, they make a decision based on the same sort of thing the agency uses when it creates advertising—*intuition*—a gut feeling about the people and the place and the way the people in the place work together to get the job done. Even though clients know that's a perfectly reasonable way to make a decision, and they realize it's how most important decisions are made, they still don't like it. Like the rest of us, they still crave certainty.

After the decision is made and the chosen agency gets to know enough about the client's business to create advertising, the agency presents its new work.

The client is shocked. The work is so, well, so . . . way out! So original! So . . . noticeable! Suddenly the president is beginning to feel sort of . . . overexposed. The work that was good because the agency said it was good suddenly doesn't look so good, even though the agency says it's great. In fact, it looks almost . . . *threat*ening. The advertising committee retires to the executive conference room, where they ask each other whether what they've bought is really what they *thought* they were buying. Now that the work is no longer theoretical, now that they're being asked to actually pay to *produce* it, well, they're not so sure anymore.

Phrases like "Let's see what the guys upstairs have to say about this" echo through headquarters. Someone asks what the chairman might think of it. Suddenly someone else remembers that the chairman once expressed distaste for red—or was it blue, or yellow, or pictures of horned animals? Anyway, it was something that's an integral part of this flashy new work the new agency insists is good enough to run. A bright young lad suggests they check out what the competition is doing. An assistant to the assistant ad director is dispatched to round it all up. They stare at it, asking themselves whether their work should really be so different from what everybody else is doing, which is pretty much what they themselves were doing until this flashy new stuff showed up. Is this new stuff really *us*? somebody asks. A guy with rimless glasses and an engineering background looks up from his computer keyboard and suggests they test it. Yeah! That's good idea, let's test it! No sense going off half-cocked when X number of millions are involved!

The agency is called in. "Who told you to go off half-cocked and do work like that, so weird and frightening and off the wall?" they are asked in so many words. "How do you know it will work?"

"Our intuition tells us it will work," they reply. "That's our business—intuition."

"Well," the client answers, "we'll have to see about that." The agency is told to go home and have dinner while the client burns the midnight oil thinking about it some more. At midnight it is decided that intuition isn't enough unless it is backed by . . . *research*! It is requested that the agency test all this weird stuff and report back ASAP.

Meanwhile, it is officially requested, in black and white right there on the account executive's meeting report, that the agency show the client some backup stuff that's more like what the old agency (the one they fired) used to do for them in the bad old days before all the management reshuffles and the mega-mergers. The glimmer of doubt that has begun to appear is now only a small glow, but anything less than a phenomenally high twenty-four-hour recall test score for the flashy stuff is likely to fan it into an intense flame. If they test the flashy stuff against the tamer, safer backup stuff, and the tame stuff wins or the scores are about equal, that will be reason enough for everybody to forget about glitz and flash and making a splash.

So when all is said and done, what the new client winds up with is new stuff done by the new agency that is very much like the tired, predictable stuff the old, fired agency gave them.

The moral? Whether advertising is created by two guys with plaid sport jackets named Moe and Lou who chomp cigars in a storefront on the corner, or by geniuses in Armani suits on the highest floor of the tallest building in town, advertising, any kind of advertising, is based on intuition, hunch, and educated guess. If you don't have the stomach for it—if you want something that you can be absolutely certain testing will prove to be "the right stuff" in every sense of the word—you should not waste a lot of time selecting the agency that showed you the brightest and most innovative creative work. You should go with the one that showed you the longest, best-thumbed list of advertising testing services.

Unfortunately, for some reason words like *intuition* tend to make businesspeople who are spending millions of dollars on advertising uneasy. Never mind that DeWitt Wallace started *The Reader's Digest* and that Henry Luce started *Time* and *Fortune* (during the Depression, no less) on a hunch. Never mind that Steve Jobs and Steve Wozniak had a hunch that cute little personal computers that were easy for the average Joe to work would catch on. Never mind that Sony's chairman, Akio Morita, had a hunch that tiny little FM stereo radios that people had to listen to through headphones would find a ready market.

These days, it seems, every client who spends more than thirty-five dollars a year on advertising has a guy on staff whose job is to come to work and scare everybody in the company out of his wits. He sits six inches behind each person who evaluates advertising and whispers in his ear: "What if we get a letter from somebody *complaining* about this witty new advertising? What if a couple of people in every thousand don't fully under*stand* it? What if the fellas at the country club *laugh* at this stuff behind our backs? What then? I mean, can you be absolutely *sure* these sharpies at the agency really know what they're talking about? Who *are* they, anyway? They're only the *agency. They* work for *us*, dammit! We can fire their ass *any time we want,* for Chrissake, because, well, the fact of the matter is, when you think about it, they're really nothing more than . . . suppliers! Forty-five storyboards are really nothing more than thirty-three hundred pounds of nails or forty-five hundred pounds of coil springs, right? Sure. I bet our chairman doesn't even know their chairman's first name!"

The main reason you hire any agency is that you trust their intuition, which is the basis of their creative judgment. Learn to rely on it and accept the risks involved in buying the kind of work the agency tries to sell you the first time they present to you. That represents their most inspired work, the work they are most sure of, the work that's bound to work best for you. The risks involved in trusting their judgment are small, when you consider the risks and economic waste involved in paying for advertising that nobody notices or remembers, because it looks just like everybody else's advertising.

# SMALL CAN BE BEAUTIFUL

## 10

The smaller your ads are, the simpler the layouts should be and the cleaner the ads should look. If you lack money for photos, the agency art director can make all-type ads work for you. The same principles that apply to word–picture combinations apply to type. Certain styles of type give off certain implicit emotional messages. Some type is "warm," some "cold but authoritative," some "playful," and so forth. Large type set against smaller type, and properly contrasted black and white spaces, can be very dramatic.

Of course, the headline must be very intriguing if there's no picture to help it. Try not to use subheadlines in small ads. If your headline needs a subhead, either to amplify or to clarify it, ask your agency to write a headline that's more direct. If they can't, rethink the message you want your ad to deliver. Maybe you need two different ads.

By the way, *intriguing* does not necessarily mean cutesy or vague. A clever, witty headline can be quite direct, even if it has a double meaning. In Chapter 16, where I critique excellent published ads, I've reprinted some first-rate examples of small space ads.

The most basic mistake clients with small budgets make has less to do with what's in the ads than with the care and preparation, or lack of it, that go into creating the creative strategy. The first thing you have to do is decide what you've got to sell. Then you must figure out what you want to say and whom you want to say it to. Finally, you must decide where and how frequently you can afford to say it. It's your agency's creative department's job to tell you *how* to say it.

Let's say you own a hotel and you want to advertise it. Since the heart of any ad campaign is a benefit, you have to isolate the specific benefits your hotel offers the travelers you want to reach. Your hotel's benefits are either tangible—good food, convenient location, ample room size, convenient registration and bill payment and so forth—or intangible—quality of service, prestige, and the like. Although each ad may dramatize a different benefit, or the same benefit in a slightly different way, the series of ads that constitutes the entire campaign should get across the idea that your hotel stands for *one* characteristic or feature or *one* overall benefit that you offer guests, that no other hotel can offer to quite the same degree. Whatever that benefit is, it can be referred to or summed up in the campaign tag line at the bottom of each ad, and in a paragraph or a line or two of copy in each ad.

If your ads are tastefully laid out and the headline–visual combinations are provocative, readers thumbing through a magazine will notice them. They may even read part of the copy, or all of it, if you keep it short. As the months go by, they'll begin to associate your hotel with the main theme of your campaign. They'll think of your hotel as a "well-advertised" place that people in the know have heard about. It will no longer be a brand-X, anonymous also-ran that travelers are afraid to try because they don't know anything about it.

When you evaluate the advertising your agency recommends, remember that small pictures of big things—crowds of smiling, well-dressed people eating, for example—are dull. One group of happy people looks exactly like any other group of happy people. By the same token, pictures of the chef or major domo are meaningless unless the ad is about what that person does especially well that benefits the hotel's guests. *Big* pictures of *small* things can be quite effective in small adds. Don't insist on a picture of your hotel in your ad—remember, small pictures of big objects are not especially dramatic. Above all, *use words and pictures to dramatize your specific benefit in a specific way.* Don't be vague. A picture of two pieces of chocolate on a pillow says a lot more about great service than a picture of a smiling waiter or bellhop.

Try to think of specific incidents that illustrate the benefits your hotel offers. Make sure each of your ads tells a story about your hotel instead of simply making a statement or a claim about it. People who check into hotels experience many deeply felt emotions—a sense of familiarity and security when they lock the door to their room; a sense that they're in control of a predictable environ-ment if the hotel is part of a well-known chain; a feeling that they're important and about to have an especially good time if they're in a classy, expensive hotel. It's the job of your advertising to tap into these emotions in order to attract the reader's attention.

Before you give your agency a single directive, before a single ad is written, it is your job as an advertiser to organize and categorize your thinking about your hotel, and to try to be objective about what it does and does not offer.

Bear in mind that the magazine readers and TV viewers couldn't care less about you, what you do for a living, or what you have to offer them that you claim will improve their lives. Many of the elements of your business or service that you're proudest of, the accomplishments you've fought long and hard for, mean absolutely nothing to an uninterested observer. Don't force your agency to cre-ate ads that dwell on details and features nobody cares about. They will only detract from the essence of the story you *do* have to tell.

Whether you are advertising a university, a bank, a restaurant, a nursing home, or a retail store—indeed, any product or service whose ad budget is small—the guidelines I've outlined should help you help your agency create effective ad-vertising for you. But you must have faith in the agency you've picked to do the job, and you must manifest your trust and confidence in their talent, taste, and judgment from the moment you sign a contract with them. Many small adver-tisers who have not had a great deal of experience with ad agencies remain distrustful. No matter how hard the agency tries to gain their confidence, they remain wary. They make lots of inconsequential changes in every ad at the last minute. When legitimate areas of disagreement crop up, they try to get their way by bullying the agency. They waste the agency's time and energy with petty arguments about production costs. If you don't trust the agency you've picked, tell them frankly that you're not comfortable with them. Then pick another shop that you feel you can treat as a business partner, and stick with them.

If my advice to small advertisers sounds a lot like the advice I've offered large advertisers, that's because it is. Advertising is advertising; the thinking behind effective advertising, and the proper attitude to maintain toward your agency, remain the same no matter how much or how little money you're spending. Advertising, properly conceived and properly executed, works. What screws it up is the people who do not understand the nature of the process.

One other bit of advice, which I have also given to large advertisers, bears re-peating: Don't expect even the best ads to work miracles. Good advertising must be followed up by good product performance over a period of time in order for word of mouth (the most effective kind of advertising) to spread. Agencies en-thusiastically competing for your business may tend to overpromise, giving you the impression that advertising is the key to overnight success. Don't be misled—it can take many weeks, even months, of running consistently excellent advertising, which skillfully dramatizes your product's key benefits and artfully sums up what it has to offer, before you'll be able to see results.

# CORPORATE ADVERTISING: HOW TO AVOID PUTTING YOUR AUDIENCE TO SLEEP EVEN THOUGH YOU HAVE NOTHING VERY IMPORTANT TO TELL THEM

## 11

I have never been able to figure out why so many corporations spend so much money to advertise themselves. I'm told the real targets of many of these campaigns are the stockholders, the stockbrokers, the company's employees, or all three. I seriously doubt that sophisticated audiences turn to ads for accurate and reliable information about how a company is being managed or what kind of future it's likely to have. But I do think that excellent corporate advertising can increase the frequency and intensity of positive feelings the public has toward a company—and the better the public, or any part of it, feels about a company, the easier it should be for that company to make its way in the world.

Most corporate advertising, however, doesn't work very well because it lacks *news* and it lacks *tension*. The primary reason for that, in my opinion, is that the people in top management who approve it are too close to it.

As I pointed out in the last chapter, it is very difficult for most of us to promote ourselves aggressively. Even ad agencies, who are supposed to be expert at promotion, rarely win creative awards for their house ads. The problem is even greater for corporate management, because they are spending large amounts of somebody else's money to promote a large, amorphous organization with a great many attributes, to an unseen audience of millions of people who have no direct contact with that organization. To make matters worse, logic would seem to dictate that a large company, spending a large sum to press its point upon the public, should talk about something weighty, something of great moment. Naturally, when one speaks of weighty matters—the principles on which the company was founded, the truths it holds dear, the American Way of Life, Integrity, Democracy, Freedom, Life, Liberty, the Pursuit of Happiness, and so forth—it seems logical that one should speak in a weighty way.

Unfortunately, to many corporate managers, speaking in a weighty way means depicting what they want to say with abstract images and intangible symbols. Thumbing through *Fortune* or *Forbes* one comes across one corporate ad after another featuring prominent illustrations of intertwined strands of steel cable twirling through the sky (symbolizing strength and durability), disembodied hands reaching toward stars (symbolizing ambition), outlines of a blank human body with a red glow where the brain should be (symbolizing humankind or intellectual skills), and so forth. Abstract pictures and photos require headlines that explain them. It is very hard to begin to tell a story that will interest ordinary consumers if you begin with an abstraction that you have to explain. Remember the fairy tales we grew up with? Most of them began with "Once upon a time . . ." and immediately went into detail about the adventures of powerful kings, beautiful princesses, wicked witches, mysterious wizards, princely frogs, and the like. There was nothing abstract about them. That was what made them so engrossing.

Popular stories, whether they concern fairies, products, or corporate points of view, always use concrete images and are always about specific people doing recognizable things in locales with which ordinary audiences can identify. The more down to earth the words and pictures in your corporate advertising, the more likely your audience is to be attracted to them. The more vague and intangible your headline–visual combination, the less likely they are to be interested.

To give you an example of what I'm talking about, I'd like to ask you a question: Assuming your state runs a lottery, what would you do if you won it? Think about it for a moment.

What thoughts came to mind? Did you think of abstractions—college courses you could take to improve your mind, books you could read to add meaning to your life? Or did you think of concrete things—trips to Hong Kong or Alaska or Europe, cars, houses, jewelry, clothes, and so forth? Chances are you thought of specific items you could buy. You did not try to visualize the *idea* of being a winner; your fantasies involved specific things you could use immediately.

Bear that in mind when you evaluate corporate advertising. Also bear in mind that, since the reader or viewer of corporate advertising will not be rewarded with information about a tangible benefit, the reward for paying attention must be in the reading or viewing itself. That makes it especially vital that the headlines and visuals in print ads, and the action, music, and voice track in corporate TV commercials, dramatize the corporate point of view in an especially provocative way.

The typical top corporate manager's carefully cultivated sense of professional reserve, especially when talking about something as close to himself as his company, and the agency's creative people's exuberant sense of theater and preoccupation with drama and impact, are at opposite poles. When the two meet head on, the result is predictable. The agency account people wind up imploring the creatives to "address the client's reservations." To the creative people, this is usually a euphemism for watering down the advertising so that it is less interesting, less exciting, safer, more predictable, and ultimately less fun to look at or read.

Is there a way out of this bind? Definitely. If corporate management is to communicate effectively with masses of people through advertising media, they must begin by taking pains to distance themselves from their own advertising, so they can view it objectively.

The first step is to examine half a dozen current corporate campaigns, including, if possible, some run by companies in direct competition with yours. Make separate groupings of three or four ads in each campaign. Write down in ten or fifteen words exactly what you think each of the campaigns is trying to tell readers. Then, in one paragraph under each fifteen-word grouping, describe how the message has been executed.

Chances are, most of the ads will look like conventional, generic corporate advertising; they will be long-winded, vague, flat, and dull, because most corporate advertising is long-winded, vague, flat, and dull. Decide which campaigns fail and which succeed and to what degree they succeed. Write a paragraph of no more than twenty-five words explaining your decision. Place it next to the other two groupings. Then meet with your agency account and creative people and discuss your conclusions.

Earlier I mentioned the words *news and tension*. It is all well and good if your corporate advertising contains genuine news, but few corporate campaigns do. That is not necessarily a problem, because advertising that is executed in an interesting way is, of itself, newsworthy. To the average reader or viewer, a moment of stimulation is a moment of stimulation; he does not care whether an ad attracts his attention because of what it says or how it says it.

A word about *tension*: A dramatist creates interest by creating a sense of tension in his audience. By setting the scene and moving the action forward through dialogue in such a way that tension begins to build, he keeps his audience interested. In the same manner, sculptors are expert at creating tension through ostensibly static figures. For example, what makes the sculpture of Giacometti so interesting is not that his pieces look a lot like a child's stick figures, but that they seem to embody tension—a reaching out, a breaking through of individual isolation in an attempt to communicate, and at the same time a withdrawal, a retreat inward. His figures speak to us so powerfully as metaphors for life in the twentieth century because to some degree we all suffer the ambivalence that comes with craving intimacy on the one hand and fearing the vulnerability we experience when we expose our innermost feelings on the other.

To be successful, the headline–visual combination in corporate print advertising, and the way the copy and visuals relate in corporate TV, must create a feeling of tension in the audience. When, figuratively speaking, a member of the audience asks himself, "What exactly are they getting at by using that headline with that photograph?" what they are really expressing is a sense of tension—tension that is aroused by the curious, perhaps even slightly mysterious, connection between the words and the picture.

Recently I came across a full-page corporate ad for Raytheon in *The Wall Street Journal*. At the top was a large picture of a fishing yacht under full power heading across the bow of a supercarrier. The contrast between the immense carrier and the much smaller boat made the picture interesting. The headline read, "What they have in common could keep them apart." The copy pointed out that both vessels used radar made by Raytheon. The nicely written headline combined with the provocative picture led the reader to ask, "Just what is it that these two completely different vessels have in common? There certainly can't be much!" Although the ad took up the entire *Journal* page, there were less than 175 words of copy. Surrounding seven paragraphs of copy with all that white space made the copy seem short and easy to read.

The tension advertising strives to create and make use of is similar to the tension a magician arouses in his audience when he sets out to perform a stunt. The audience is confident that the girl will float in the air seemingly unaided, or that the elephant or the tiger will disappear before their very eyes, since they've seen the trick before. But that doesn't matter. They stare at the performer, trying to catch him while he's trying to trick them, and when they fail and he succeeds, they are delighted. In effect, the tension made up partly of the hope he will succeed in fooling them and partly out of the fear that he will be humiliated should he fail, is actually relieved when he pulls the trick off perfectly. Magicians know that though audiences always ask them to reveal the secret behind a trick, they don't really want to know, because the knowledge would eliminate the tension, and therefore the fun.

Corporate advertising that works, like product advertising that works, creates a slight bit of tension in the audience to whom it is first exposed. And like all the old jokes about Jack Benny's stinginess, a successful commercial or print ad works over and over again, even though the audience has figured out the meaning of the provocative headline/visual combination after their first exposure to the print ad, and in the case of a TV commercial, it has learned what's coming at the end of the commercial. For months, audiences who watched Wendy's "Where's the beef" spots laughed or smiled each time they saw and heard Clara Peller demand to know where the beef was. Freud pointed out that laughter is the release of tension. Each time one of those spots appeared, consumers experienced the slight buildup and release of tension that resulted in a chuckle.

Successful corporate advertising, like successful product advertising, must contain some sort of built-in tension producer. In other words, a successful execution of the corporate advertising strategy must possess some unusual twist, some conceptual or executional element or device that comes as a surprise and makes the advertising seem novel to the audience. The closer the corporate advertising executions are to straightforward, literal speeches, or sequential displays of well-reasoned arguments, or declarations of solemn corporate credos, the less successful they are likely to be.

# THE COLOSSAL ADVERTISER, OR:

# THE RICH ARE DIFFERENT FROM

# YOU AND ME

## 12

At this point, you may be thinking: "What you say seems to make sense. But how do you explain all the big budget TV campaigns I see, especially those for beer and soft drinks, that don't seem to make use of any storytelling techniques I can think of? They don't seem very specific to me, and no matter how I search for a product benefit that's being dramatized, I can't seem to find any. While you keep preaching that the best advertising is simple, many of these spots seem anything but. They're full of so many quick cuts of so many different people doing so many different things, I can hardly count them, let alone try to figure out what one, simple selling message the spots are trying to give me. Obviously, these campaigns must work, because sophisticated, successful advertisers have spent hundreds of millions of dollars on them over the years. What gives?"

The basic creative guidelines that work for small advertisers also work for very large advertisers. But when it comes to advertisers who spend, say $50 million to $100 million or more annually on a single product, the differences of extent can become so great that, in some respects, they border on being differences of kind.

To begin with, the largest of the beer, soft drink, and fast food chains have virtually become national institutions. Consumers actually formed groups and wrote letters of protest when Coke changed their formula. For a short period, Pepsi used 1984 vice-presidential candidate Geraldine Ferarro as a spokeswoman. These products are so much a part of consumers' daily lives, and their commercials are so much a part of major sports events and America's weekly evening entertainment, that words like *news, tension, drama,* and *surprise* have to be seen in a broader context than those that apply to the typical advertiser. (The large fast food chains do have genuine news about new menu items to offer viewers from time to time. But broadly speaking, the major fast food chains as well as the nation's most popular beers and soft drinks remain the same products they've always been.)

Most of the advertising for these types of products comes under the heading of "life-style." Since few of these products offer a specific benefit the competition lacks, the theory is that the best way to promote them is to make them part of a scene involving music and good-looking young people drinking or eating or using the products while they celebrate life with friends and family. The thought (and the hope) is that if the spots are attractive and interesting enough, they will not only remind consumers in the target audience of the product's existence, but will plant the thought in their minds that it is a contemporary product or, to use the current ad jargon, a product with "currency." As Ogilvy group director Peter Barnet put it, "You try to get them to say, 'This is my kind of product for my kind of people. It's the choice of a lot of people with whom I identify, who I would like to emulate, and who seem to enjoy life in a way with which I empathize.'"

A friend of mine who is an agency creative head told me: "It is the *attitude* the advertising conveys about the product that is key to a campaign's success. If you can convey the right attitude, sometimes it can be as simple as not taking oneself or not appearing to take the product you're advertising too seriously—and when that attitude hits a nerve in your target audience, you've got a hit. You can build a brand on an attitude or a tag line, although just as often the tag line doesn't matter because nobody remembers it. We're good at it. But don't ask me to analyze it. All I can tell you is, it's good advertising, but a different kind of good advertising than, say, BMW or Honda advertising, where you've really got something specific to talk about and can do the quote-unquote heavy concept stuff."

When it comes to life-style advertising, the line between the movie, TV, and music businesses and the advertising business often disappears entirely. Movie sound tracks sound like commercials, which sound like movies, which sound like MTV tracks. At times, commercials actually parody popular movies and TV series. Pepsi ran a thirty-second take-off of the hit movie *Top Gun.* They also ran a "Miami Vice" take-off, directed by the well-known movie director Ridley Scott, that featured Don Johnson and his Ferrari.

Many creative people disparage life-style advertising. They insist it fails to sell well because it often lacks a strong selling idea. They feel that because it lacks meat, it lacks force. Former Doyle Dane Bernbach creative chief Roy Grace, who now heads his own firm, Grace & Rothschild, told a *New York Times* reporter, "Production values are trying to take the place of ideas." In his view, such commercials are nothing more than "beautifully produced garbage, fancy fluff."

Two acknowledged masters of the life-style commercial are Bill Backer, vice-chairman and executive creative director of Backer Spielvogel Bates Worldwide, and Phil Dusenberry, chairman and chief creative officer of BBDO Worldwide. They have created some of the most popular and successful life-style advertising campaigns of recent years. Backer and his people are responsible for the famous "I'd like to buy the world a Coke and keep it company" commercial, with kids of various nationalities singing the song atop a grass-covered hill. It was so well received, it became a popular song ("We just took the word 'Coke' out of it and wrote a middle eight bridge," Bill explained). Bill and his staff also created "Now comes Miller Time," and "Everything you always wanted in a beer and less," for Miller Lite.

Speaking of the work he used to do for Coke, Bill told me:

We used to write those songs and give them out to various art directors around the agency for ways of staging them. We used to tell them, "Don't do show and tell pictures." The pictures should amplify a piece of music, they shouldn't say the same thing as the music. [Just as the visual in a print ad should amplify rather than simply decorate the headline whenever possible.] They shouldn't say anything contradictory, of course. The film can add elements that the lyrics don't specifically talk about."

Bill believes the same homely truths and deeply felt human needs that are expressed in spirituals and folk songs lie behind the music in good life-style advertising. And he feels that, to be successful, this type of advertising must come directly out of the product. He told me:

The best of these things, whether folk songs or the best of the life-style type of songs, are grounded on something very solid—about the product, about its appeal, about how it relates to people—as long as they don't stretch credibility too far. The songs tap real emotions—sunshine, people getting together and talking about their problems, relating to each other while drinking the product, that's one of the real things that makes the world go round.

For example, his idea for "I'd like to buy the world a Coke" came from watching a large bunch of angry, stranded plane passengers of many nationalities and ethnic backgrounds in Shannon Airport gradually become friendly after several days of sitting around and talking to each other over coffee and Cokes. As Bill said:

Coke had a unique selling proposition right in that song. What makes all the great campaigns work is that they are based upon a USP (unique selling proposition). Coke was the only soft drink that could say "It's the real thing." It was the first, original cola. Everything we did was always based on a claim or an attitude about the product that we could try to franchise as our own. If you can run it awhile, you can own it.

The best of those things is "Marlboro Country." You could have gone out and had "Winston Country" first, but since they didn't, Marlboro was able to build a USP or franchise. Ideally, it's better to start with one, but if you don't, you can come up with one. McDonald's did "You deserve a break today," because they were the leader. Quite frequently the leader can franchise something the others can't. They can take what is or was the generic reason for going out to dinner. When everybody was going out, it gave Mom a little break from eating at home. It was the generic appeal for all inexpensive, eat-out little places.

Bill admires the current Pepsi advertising very much:

Pepsi knows what it wants to be; the choice of the next generation. That has validity, because the sweeter, less sharp taste of Pepsi is more appealing to young people than Coke's. It has a little more sugar and a little less carbonation and a little less phosphoric acid. It's not as dry a taste as Coca Cola.

I think that a song that says, like the Bud song does, "Hey, you're working your ass off and for all you do, the king of beers comes through for you," is both emotional and there's a USP under it. It's extremely well grounded in something that songs sing about. . . .

Bud's been pushing "the king of beers" for years, so when it says the king of beers is going to come through for you, that might embarrass beer drinkers a little bit, about being the king and so forth. But the truth is, Bud's the leading beer. Only they can say that. It wouldn't be believable coming from anybody else.

Like Phil Dusenberry, Bill is contemptuous of most of the life-style work currently on the air:

Eighty percent of what you see on the air today is singing about product specs. They use hip young language, and put what they think are hip, techniquey pictures to 'em. And it's the delight of many clients to be hip and put nice, flat colors against it, to make it look like a little MTV thing. . . .

Many of the vignettes in these commercials are all the same. All the top directors know how to shoot 'em. All you have to do is go back to the same location, give it a slightly different angle or a different character. I've often thought it would be a very good business for somebody to have a business called "rent a vignette." You could do a collection of generic vignettes and sell them to different advertisers. . . .

Phil Dusenberry and his staff created the classic "We bring good things to life" campaign for GE. It won numerous creative awards and helped revitalize the company's image. Top creative and account people who work on similar accounts, and know how difficult it is to create a breakthrough advertising for what are essentially parity products, express great admiration for the wit, daring, and flair Phil and his people have demonstrated in their work for Pepsi over the last several years. BBDO has created a number of award-winning spots that have poked fun at the competition in a friendly, lighthearted way. Dusenberry points out that humorous executions require great care. "We do it with a light touch," he told me. "People will laugh along with you, and enjoy it and they won't mind it, if you do it in a friendly way, with humor, and if the spot doesn't take itself too seriously. You can still make a valid point. But if what you do is heavyhanded, there'll be a backlash."

If it is to succeed, life-style advertising requires an especially trusting, confident, patient client, because the production and media costs are enormous and the payoff, though potentially huge, is not immediate. Plus, if the commercial bombs for some reason and Johnny Carson and David Letterman begin making jokes about it, or if the celebrity used in a commercial is unexpectedly arrested for drunk driving or dealing drugs, the client runs the risk of being embarrassed before the entire nation.

Finally, since the audience is so enormous, changing their attitudes and perceptions takes a lot of time. "Life-style advertising, more than any other kind, needs time to work and to flower and flourish," Phil told me. "It's not a one-night stand, not a quick hit."

In sum, effective life-style campaigns provide products with enhanced value. The buyer not only gets the bottle of beer or the can of soda, he gets the extra bit of cachet, that fragment of a dream, that angelic halo that makes one product more valuable, more desirable, than all the others. The label becomes a flag that reads, "Buy me and, for a few blissful moments, I will help you be the better person you have always dreamed of being, who lives the kind of life you have always dreamed of living."

On the other hand, there is a category of commercials that work well simply because they're cute or because there's something about the particular combination of songs and visuals that is catchy enough to attract attention in a limited period, the way certain popular songs do.

The brilliant English director Ridley Scott shot the completely surreal, stark-looking "Share the Fantasy" Chanel No. 5 commercial, which went on the air in 1979 and ran unchanged for five years. A second, equally surreal spot ran nearly three years. The first spot, with the old tune "I Don't Want To Set The World On Fire" sung on the track, features shots of an estate, piano keys, a train, a plane, a man in an office tower, a young woman walking into the office, a passing plane reflected on the side of an office tower, and other scenes. The second spot featured another estate, and a young woman in a gown who slips it off, revealing a bathing suit as she walks by the side of a pool. She kicks her shoe into the pool. A handsome man dives into the pool, retrieves her shoe, swims to her end of the pool, and hands it to her. He disappears. The shadow of a passing plane sweeps across the scene. The man disappears, and then the woman disappears.

An elaborate new spot, also shot by Ridley Scott, began running in December 1987. It featured Carole Bouquet, an actress new to Chanel. The song in this spot was "My Baby Just Cares For Me," sung by Nina Simone. The actress was shown on a high floor of a Houston office building. She gave an older man a peck on the forehead, drove a high-priced black car into the desert, got gas, was leered at by the young man who gave her gas, drove to Monument Valley and met a man who was apparently the one she was looking for. She kissed him. In wonderfully weird, primitive, and completely inexplicable ways, the symbolism in these commercials, which seems to be largely sexual, works.

Some campaigns are hard to pigeonhole. They seem to lie somewhere in the limbo between life-style and vignette-with-song. They do not seek to convey a specific message. Rather, they provide an inspirational umbrella or motif for every piece of publicity, advertising, and promotion some large advertisers do. When they're successful, they galvanize the company's efforts and add a certain liveliness to its image in a way that probably could not be duplicated with more conventional spots. Chrysler's excellent series of vignettes featuring Kenny Rogers singing "The Pride Is Back—Born In America" served as a kind of flag or standard bearer for all of Chrysler's advertising efforts. To some degree, Chevrolet's beautifully produced "Heartbeat Of America" commercials did the same thing.

There's an old saying in the ad business, "When you have nothing to say, sing it." Some banks, insurance companies, and hotel chains (and, I must admit, some agencies) who do not understand the value, strength, and risks involved in life-style advertising and the vast budgets needed to make it work properly, tend to rush pell mell into it, even though it is not appropriate for their product or service. Many advertisers, convinced a great jingle will do for them what Backer and Dusenberry and their people have done for Pepsi and Miller, waste precious dollars on silly, elaborately produced, song-filled spots that offer the consumer next to no information about what the advertiser offers or why they should try the product he offers.

Sad to say, agencies frequently encourage clients to charge down this blind path. After all, it's fun to shoot commercials full of beautiful young people on location. It's glamorous. And most important, it's easy and, in the short-term, highly profitable. Manhattan, L.A., and Chicago are filled with talented free-lance songwriters and directors who are talented shooters. If the agency lacks copywriters and art directors talented enough to come up with executional concepts that contain heart and substance, who's the wiser? For a one-time fee, the songwriter will make the flight of spots sound wonderful, and the shooter will make them look good. If the campaign fails to make a dent in the public mind after a year or two—because at heart it's basically inauthentic and lightweight—who can blame the agency? Advertising is subjective and unpredictable, right? Taking the easy way out beats spending weeks digging into the client's background and studying his business in depth in order to come up with an executional concept that is not only bright and fresh, but also tailor made to solve his ad problems.

In my opinion, it is the derivative, inappropriate, mediocre life-style advertising we see so frequently on TV that gives the best of the genre a bad name. I believe it is this kind of work that people like Roy Grace have in mind when they criticize the life-style technique.

The advertiser who wonders whether life-style is the way to go should bear a few things in mind: First, it takes a peculiar kind of brilliance on your agency's part to do it right. If they haven't done it before, for somebody else, I would seriously question whether they can do it for you. Second, on the whole, it takes a lot of time and a lot of money to make life-style work the way it's supposed to, so you must be prepared for some serious spending. Third, as both Bill Backer and Phil Dusenberry take pains to point out, although great life-style advertising like Budweiser's and Miller's may seem glib, slick, superficial, and easy to imitate on the surface, it is anything but. It works as well as it does because, in inexplicable but powerful ways, the mix of its elements taps deeply held emotions and beliefs in the target audience. Finally, don't decide to go with life-style unless you trust your agency's intuition and sense of showmanship implicitly, because no "copy research" can tell you whether or not it's going to work before the fact, any more than research can tell a movie or record company whether its efforts will pay off in the marketplace before the movie is made or the song is sung. The best you can do in the tea leaf–reading department is to put the spot on the air, wait awhile, and track it to see how it's doing.

What makes the quality and effectiveness of life-style advertising so difficult to judge, up close, is that sometimes the cumulative effect of successful advertising of this kind can be much greater than the effect of any one commercial. For example, although many people in the industry are not crazy about every single Pepsi spot, few would argue that the campaign as a whole has added a spirit of freshness and fun to the brand image of what for generations had been an old-fashioned, runner-up soda pop. Clever marketing and lively, entertaining advertising has turned Pepsi into the kind of product that fashionable, attractive, socially active young people enjoy drinking.

# THINGS THAT GO BUMP IN THE NIGHT:

# COMMON CLIENT SUPERSTITIONS

## 13

1. *Always put the product name and benefit in the headline, because 85 percent of the people don't read body copy.*

I have often heard this 85 percent figure quoted. Several years ago, when I was writing a column for *Advertising Age,* I spent many hours trying to substantiate it. I couldn't.

Logic dictates that many more people will read headlines than body copy, since headlines are shorter, set in larger type, and usually accompanied by pictures. How many more people? That depends on many factors. There's certainly no sensible way to come up with any sort of meaningful average. When people quote the 85 percent figure, I always ask, 85 percent of what kind of people, reading what kind of ads—black-and-white trade ads? Color ads? Detergent ads in women's magazines? Fashion ads? Cosmetic ads? The copy in a Corvette or Porsche 928 ad is bound to be more interesting to readers, especially male readers, and therefore more likely to be read all the way through, than copy about prosaic products like catsup, toilet tissue, tires, tacks, or house paint.

Whether or not the product or the benefit is mentioned in the headline, provocative headline–visual combinations will entice more readers into reading the copy than dull combinations will. Personally, I'd rather have fewer readers read my ad all the way through, spending one or two minutes with it, than have many more readers simply glance at my long, leaden headline-equipped-with-a-benefit-and-a-product-name for half a second before moving on. Those readers who stay with the ad longer are more likely to remember the product and have positive feelings toward it than the many readers who barely notice a boring ad's headline–visual combination.

2. *For best results, show the product in use.*

Not necessarily. What you must try to do in print and on TV is to show the product in a dramatic way. It doesn't matter whether it's shown in use or in limbo, against a blank background. The finest ad photographers and cinematographers can make almost any product look fascinating. To an expert, there's no such thing as a dull-looking product, especially when the illustration or photograph is accompanied by an interesting headline.

3. *Showing my product with people helps personalize and "warm up" my advertising, making it more appealing to consumers.*

It's true that people are more interested in other people than in anything else. But it's not necessarily true that showing people with your product warms up your advertising and makes it more interesting to viewers in general.

The biggest problem with this rule is that it leads to clichés. If all your competitors use people in their ads, then the best way to get attention for your ads may be to *eliminate* people from them. Some of the best foreign car advertising in the last twenty-five years—Volvo, BMW, Saab, Subaru, Honda, and VW—almost never shows people with the cars in print ads, unless the people have something to do with the headline and the creative concept of the ad. The great "Think Small" ad for VW showed a very small picture of the car near the upper-left-hand corner of the page. Placing a small picture of a car—a large object—in a sea of white space attracted far more attention to the car than would a traditional, full-sized picture, with models draped languorously over the hood. The placement of the car on the page, and the word play involved in inverting the colloquial phrase "think big," gave the ad a warm, folksy tone without using a picture of people. It attracted people's attention because it was so different from competitive ads, and it established a personality for VW that helped sell the car to a whole generation of Americans who, according to the prevailing wisdom of the time, would never buy an ugly car.

4. *Copy should never be printed in reverse (white on black).*

It can be harder to read white on black than black on white. But a headline or copy set that way, because it's unusual, can also be more dramatic and attract more attention. A headline set in reverse, above type set black on white, can be an eye stopper. The point is, copy can be printed on a white background, a black background, a silver background, a gold background—any background. An ad that is provocative in a relevant, believable way is a good ad, no matter what point size the copy is set in, what type style is used, or what background it's printed on. An excellent ad for Epson computers, part of a provocative and memorable campaign, ran in *The Wall Street Journal* recently. The ad took up most of the page, but the copy was blessedly short—fewer than seventy-five words. The first three words of the copy, "Every ten seconds," were printed in reverse. The rest of the copy was black on white. Printing those three words in reverse made them work like a headline, in that they attracted the eye. But the moment you read them you were already reading the copy. Using reverse type in this novel way helped create a striking and provocative headline–visual–copy combination.

5. *Avoid showing unhappy people and negative situations; they may give the audience a negative impression of your product.*

Many of the most interesting ads and TV commercials involve negative situations; many successful humorous commercials involve gross exaggerations of negative events. A common, highly effective attention-getting device is to exaggerate the calamity that will befall the consumer who fails to buy your product.

Much of what is interesting and amusing in our lives involves negative or embarrassing situations. The most successful of the early Federal Express commercials directed by the master director of comedy, Henry Sedelmaier, are actually quite negative, even hostile. In their own gentle, imaginative way, they poke fun at the unattractive, ordinary, unenlightened people who do not use the sponsor's product.

The vast majority of TV commercials are and always have been crammed with gorgeous, sappy, smiling young families rhapsodizing over the way their lives have been enhanced by various brands of shampoos, soaps, detergents, skin creams, aspirin, cereals, jeans, pickup trucks, sports cars, and the like. If your advertising is to stand out from your competitors', it has to be different. It makes perfect sense to try to be different by depicting negative situations or using gentle parodies or spoofs. As long as your product is ultimately portrayed as offering a solution to the problem you've dramatized, the total effect of your commercial should be positive.

6. *Billboards should never contain more than seven words.*

Seldom, yes. "Never," no. Obviously, people driving past billboards do not have much time to read long copy. But millions of people pass the same billboards day after day. Each time they see a billboard, they may be able to read the rest of a message they didn't understand completely the first time. If they're stuck in traffic, they might even welcome the opportunity to read an interesting billboard with twenty or thirty words. The correct number of words for a particular billboard is the number of words that makes that billboard as provocative as possible.

*7. Photographs work better than drawings in ads.*

Nothing works better than anything else all the time. Agency writers and art directors use whatever works. So should you. Keep an open mind.

*8. Animation in TV is not as credible as live action.*

That's generally true. But it is so often *not* true that you might as well throw this rule in the same wastebasket as the rest. The recent, enormously successful claymation spots for the California Raisin Advisory Board, which showed animated fruit dancing and mouthing the lyrics of Marvin Gaye's "I Heard It Through The Grapevine," are just one example of terrific animated spots.

*9. Research shows the most effective TV commercials mention the name of the product in the first five seconds and the benefit in the first eight.*

Rubbish. Most TV spots do happen to mention the product and its benefit early on, but that's no reason to kill a great spot that doesn't. Beware of any and all research that leads to rules!

*10. Research shows that mentioning the product/benefit at least twice in every thirty-second commercial, and supering it when it's on the sound track, improves recall.*

It also leads to dull, boring, repetitive, derivative commercials that irritate viewers and fail to make friends for your product. And even if repeating the benefit does improve recall, so what? Can you prove that high recall translates into sales? Suppose, as I discussed earlier, people have to see a commercial several times in order to understand it fully, but when they do, they love it? Twenty-four- and seventy-two-hour recall tests can't measure that. Nor can they measure emotion—the most crucial element in all advertising.

*11. People don't buy from clowns.*

This is how advertisers who are afraid to use a humorous approach justify their fear. I grant you: Humor can be tricky. What is amusing to one person can be sophomoric, juvenile, or silly to another. On the other hand, as Victor Borge said, a joke is the shortest distance between two people.

The point is that humor that works in advertising is *humor that comes out of the product* and is immediately relevant to what the product does, or what failing to purchase the product will do to the consumer. To be successful, advertising must be interesting to consumers. Any device or technique that can make your advertising more interesting than your competitor's is worth considering seriously.

12. *Whenever possible, sell the benefit, not the product.*

Until about ten years ago, this was generally true. But things are more complicated nowadays, especially in TV.

In certain cases, for example, what the product does for the consumer is more or less self-evident, as it is with beer, soda, and most food products. So what advertisers often "sell," if that is the correct word, is neither the product nor the benefit, but something beyond that—a value imparted by the product's label, or the style of life a commercial attempts to make the product symbolize. In certain other cases, high-ticket cars and cameras for example, consumers are as fascinated with what the product *is* as with what it *does*. In other words, they are as interested in *how* it does what it does as they are in *what* it does.

As a result, there are no longer any hard and fast rules for what you should sell or dramatize about a given product. If research tells you consumers are interested in one particular benefit or characteristic, you can choose to dramatize that one in your advertising. Generally, however, consumers don't care what you dramatize, because they don't analyze ads. What they care about is whether the ad or commercial is interesting. Anything relevant that makes an ad more interesting makes it better. In some cases, when there appears to be little about the product that's of great interest, the agency makes something up. A good example is the wonderful Bartles & Jaymes wine cooler advertising that built the brand. These award-winning commercials dramatize neither the product nor its benefits. In the past, invented product spokespeople, usually called "continuing characters," mouthed whatever specific product benefits research indicated were of interest to the consumer. Charmin's famous "Mr. Whipple" is a good example. The Bartles & Jaymes characters go much farther than Mr. Whipple did. Their sell is so subtle and soft, and so artfully mixed with pure entertainment and amusing show-biz "hick-schtick," that it cannot be placed in any convenient category. Like Bill Backer's "teach the world to sing" Coke commercial, and the Isuzu "lying man" campaign, these ads work well because they attract attention to the product in a relevant and memorable way. Sometimes advertisers who are looking for the most productive executions have to look beyond rigid definitions of product characteristics, attributes, and benefits, and examine their audience's expectations and predilections. In some cases, what works best on TV turns out to be whatever execution registers the product name strongly and is fun to watch.

13. *I should always/never trash competitors in my advertising.*

Naming competitors in your advertising to their disadvantage—"trashing" them—is the wrong way to approach competitive advertising. Avoid bitter and openly disparaging references to the competition whenever possible. But using the actual names of your competitors in your advertising is perfectly legitimate, as long as it is done with restraint and taste. (See Chapter 16 for a few excellent examples.)

One very common problem in this area occurs when your competition does something that makes you furious, and you want to lash out at them and tell the public what rats they are. Often (especially in labor–management disputes) since such quarrels, and the ads participants use as weapons, strike the uninitiated reader as parochial and small-minded, they reflect poorly on both sides.

14. *Ads are stronger when the product name is in the headline.*

Earlier, I referred to an excellent ad for a tire, whose headline read, "It Bites When Cornered." Not long ago, I came across a similar ad for a car I'll call "Superduper 6." It, too, showed the car in a sharp turn. The headline read: "Superduper 6. It bites when cornered." This ad was not as effective as the first ad, even though the headline was virtually identical. Why?

The extra words at the beginning of the headline slowed it down, because they did not help tell or begin to tell the story that dramatized the benefit. They robbed the headline of the vigor and snap that the basic double entendre had. "It Bites When Cornered" says something about what the car *does*. The name of the car only says something, very little actually, about what the car *is*. A headline that says both what a product is and what it does is cumbersome because it takes longer to register in the consumer's mind than a headline that says only one thing, quickly and vigorously. In addition, the information conveyed by the car's name can better be conveyed elsewhere in the ad—either in the copy or in or near the tag line.

It may seem petty to argue about one word in a headline. But every ad struggles with every other ad for the consumer's attention. Anything that slows things down unnecessarily, especially at the beginning of the ad, diminishes its effectiveness.

Many clients reason that since most consumers don't read copy, it's best to get the product name in the headline, where more people will see it. But if the extra people who see it don't have a strong positive impression about the name, it doesn't do much good for them to see it. They get their positive impression from reading the ad. If the headline for the ad slows it down and makes it less likely that people will notice it and pay attention to it in the first place, then the total net effect of sticking the name of the product at the top will be negative. Remember—people buy benefits. Ads should dramatize benefits.

Of course, if a provocative headline can be written using the product name, it's perfectly reasonable to use it. There's no rule that says you *can't* use the name in the headline. If a provocative headline does contain the product name, you wind up with the best of both worlds. But if you mandate that your agency use the name in the headline, as so many clients do, they may be forced to twist and possibly weaken or even distort the headline to do it, and that will weaken the ad.

15. *I should never give my account to an agency that does not have experience in my specific product category area.*

Years ago, with fear and trepidation, Toyota gave their account to Dancer Fitzgerald Sample, a well-known packaged goods agency. Toyota, which is having a fine sales year as this is written, is still with Dancer (now, Saatchi Saatchi DFS Compton). They are so satisfied that reports in the trade press indicate Saatchi Saatchi will also do the advertising for Toyota's new line of luxury cars.

Most clients think their advertising problems are so unusual that only a few agencies can solve them successfully. But from an agency's point of view, clients are more alike than they are different. I firmly believe any good agency, given a little time to get to know the client, can handle virtually any kind of account.

It is true that certain agencies do specialize in certain areas, such as movie, real estate, fashion, toy, and cosmetic advertising. But generally speaking, if there are things your new agency has to learn in a hurry about you and your business, the chances are they will do what agencies have always done—they will buy the experience they need on the open market.

In theory, of course, it makes sense to conduct your search for a new agency only among those that have successfully serviced accounts similar to yours in the past. In practice, however, what many clients are really searching for when they seek "experience" is someone new who can deliver the same tired old advertising clichés the client and most of its competitors are used to.

16. *Agency people are inherently lazy. In order to get the best out of them, you have to lean on them constantly and push them around a bit. They maintain their edge if you keep them on edge.*

Agencies are not suppliers. They provide a service that can be as personal, and as important, as a makeup artist's is to a movie star. To do the best possible job, however, they have to feel some degree of loyalty to your company. They can't feel that way if you constantly offend their sensibilities by canceling meetings at a moment's notice or routinely keeping them waiting for hours. They won't feel loyal if you reject their work without a satisfactory explanation, or react capriciously to it.

The sad thing is that so many clients routinely bully agencies, when it is so easy and costs so little to cultivate them. A complimentary letter now and then, for example, will do wonders. Telling the creative people how much you appreciate all their hard work, even if the work isn't quite acceptable, does wonders for morale. A breakfast or lunch date with people in the agency's lower echelons helps them feel appreciated, and costs your company little or nothing.

# MUST READING FOR EVERYBODY WHO

# HAS ANYTHING TO DO WITH

# APPROVING ADVERTISING

## 14

## SEE ALL THE STAGE PLAYS YOU CAN, AND WHEN YOU SEE THEM, STUDY THEM.

The next time you see a play, pay special attention to everything the scenic designer, the director, and the actors do to direct your attention from one character to another or from one part of the stage to another. Since the audience can focus on only one thing at a time, there can be only one central point of focus. The same is true of an ad or a commercial. (That is why larding a piece of advertising with extraneous bits of information—indeed, with a single extraneous verbal or visual element—inevitably weakens it.)

Train yourself to take special notice of the way a stage set is designed and lit, which color combinations are used, how the actors are dressed, and so forth. Do the same thing when you see movies. The more observant you become, the better a judge of ads and commercials you will become. The more familiar you are with staged and filmed drama, the easier it will be for you to imagine how a storyboard will look when it is filmed.

## HOW TO TELL WHETHER YOUR ACCOUNT EXECUTIVE IS ANY GOOD

If he almost always agrees with you, and is a delight to have around, a pleasure to be around, and a fine drinking companion, I'd think seriously of asking for a replacement. A good account executive functions as an advocate, frequently for positions that are going to make you or your bosses uncomfortable. Diplomatically but firmly he should be encouraging your firm to accept more innovative, provocative advertising. This means that in one nice way or another, he's always going to be bugging you a bit. If he's doing his job, you will sometimes find him irritating.

An art director I used to work with put it best: "As far as a client is concerned, an account man who's a pleasure to have around is a mediocre account man. A good account man is a pain in the ass. And a great account man is a royal pain in the ass."

## BRILLIANT ADVERTISING IS NOT ALWAYS NECESSARY, BUT IT IS ALWAYS DESIRABLE

Advertising works best when it rides the crest of a wave. If you have a product that is timely and unique, useful to millions of people and affordable, competent advertising, in the right place, in the right amounts, and at the right time, will probably do the trick quite nicely.

What outstanding advertising can do for your product, whether or not it is unique, timely, useful, and affordable is to embed its name so deeply, and create such a warm, trusting, feeling about it, in the public mind (a half dozen examples come to mind: Federal Express, Apple, BMW, IBM, Budweiser, American Express, Volvo) that competitors will have a very rough time muscling in on your market in the future. If you want to extend the line someday, outstanding advertising can help pave the way. Outstanding advertising can make you look smart on Wall Street. And outstanding advertising can help build morale; everybody likes working for a famous company that produces a famous product and runs popular commercials.

## THE SECOND HARDEST THING IN ADVERTISING*

As an ad manager, it is your obligation as a client to tell your agency exactly what is wrong with the advertising campaigns you reject, without pussyfooting.

*The hardest thing in advertising, of course, is coming up with brilliant creative work, on time, and within budget.

It is also your obligation to press top management, so you can pin down their objections as specifically as possible. Even abstractions as vague as "the tone isn't right for us" are a step in the right direction. (In that particular case, the next question would be, "What exactly is wrong with the tone? Is it too somber? Too frivolous?" and so on.)

It requires the utmost finesse and discretion to press top management or anybody else, without making them hostile and defensive. The best way to do that is to make it clear that your aim is to help the ad agency, and you can't do that without top management's help. It's a touchy process: You must be aggressive without seeming to be, and, of course, you must know when to back off. But you can't regard yourself as a professional unless you can play this particular game very well. It's much easier to say no than yes to your agency, and to tell them top management just doesn't like the work but can't explain why. It may seem like that's no skin off your nose—all that will happen, after all, is that the agency will have to do more work, and they're used to that. But it *is* skin off your nose, because, as I have said before, agencies show their very best work the first time out. It is usually the freshest and most inspired work, created by a staff who are excited to be working for your company and whose morale is high.

Generally speaking, the more work you demand, the less innovative it becomes. After a long enough time and enough rejections from enough anonymous committees for arbitrary or unstated reasons, all you're likely to get is whatever the bewildered, frustrated, exhausted agency creative managers think you're likely to buy.

If you are one of those ad managers who has trouble articulating precisely what is wrong with creative work, don't feel too bad. Even some creative directors cannot articulate what is wrong with advertising they reject. I have always been amazed at how many creative directors get away with statements to their staff to the effect that "It just doesn't feel right to me." An equivalent comment I've often heard from clients is, "I'll know what's right when I see it." That's tantamount to a general telling his armies, "March off in all directions, and when I see where one of you is headed, I'll have a better fix on where I'd like the rest of you to go."

## DON'T BE SEDUCED BY MOVEMENT

These days, many film directors and agency producers are obsessed with "movement." If the characters in a commercial don't move, the camera must move. If neither moves very much, there must be a plethora of quick cuts. Perhaps this reflects the influence of MTV and the popularity of action adventure movies. But it is important to remember that the purpose of movies and rock video is solely to *entertain*. Advertising exists to *sell*, which means that at some point it must pause to say something important about a product or service in a way that is carefully considered and provocative enough to appeal to potential customers.

Movement attracts the eye, and modern teenagers seem perfectly comfortable with incessant, random movement in the stories they watch in movie theaters and on TV screens. But in advertising, movement for movement's sake, like humor for humor's sake, impedes the sales process. A profusion of images that fly by the viewer, combined with sung copy, can confuse consumers. Much of Henry Sedelmaier's great success is due to his locked-off camera. The lack of camera movement helps viewers focus on the words, the look, and the actions of the characters. It helps create a feeling of genuine emotion.

Agency producers refer to certain uncomplicated looking commercials disparagingly as "nothing more than talking heads." Talking heads are not necessarily dull; everything depends on what the heads are saying and how they say it. Ted Koppel of ABC's "Nightline" never leaves his chair, but millions of thoughtful people find him fascinating. The performance of Lieutenant Colonel Oliver North before a Senate investigating committee during the summer of 1987 was riveting to millions of Americans. Though it went on for days, for the most part, the only part of the colonel that moved was his mouth.

A year or so ago, I watched a documentary TV broadcast of the filming of Arthur Miller's *Death of a Salesman* for TV. Dustin Hoffman played Willy Loman. Most people think this is a realistic play, but the story actually unfolds as a series of dream sequences in which fact, in real time, mixes with fantasy, memory, illusion, and impression in the principal character's mind. Miller, Hoffman, and the director, Volker Schloendorff, understood that trying to make the scenery look "real" for TV would cheapen and distort the play's mood. At one point, when he talked about the scenery that was created especially for the TV shoot, which was an intriguing mixture of realistic props and impressionistic backdrops, Schloendorff explained to Hoffman that it was "the words of the play that are the play—if you concentrate the audience's attention on the scenery, you will lose the words, and it is the words that the play is about. The words, the actors, will build the play in the audience's mind."

When they filmed the scene in which Willy's son Biff discovers Willy philandering with a blond in a Boston hotel room, you could see the script girl and several members of the cast crying as they watched.

If we are to be able to create the greatest number of the strongest selling impressions for the smallest sums of money, we must increase our reliance on and appreciation for *the word*. In the last analysis, the word is all we have; it is what moves us to love, to think, to learn, to act—and, yes, to buy. If you doubt it, get hold of a videotape of *Death of a Salesman*. Or spend thirty minutes alone with The Book of Ecclesiastes.

## THE DRAWING POWER OF A STARVING WAIF

An article I came across in the April 21, 1986, issue of *Forbes* (pp. 106–107) is must reading for any ad manager. It vividly demonstrates one of the advertising principles I have stressed repeatedly: *Consumers respond to the specific, concrete, and personal* much more readily and powerfully than they do to the general, the abstract, and the impersonal.

For years, the Save the Children Federation (SCF) provided cash and clothing to poor children around the world through a one-to-one direct sponsorship approach. Donors, who got snapshots of the child they were helping, sent in money regularly and received letters from the child in return. According to *Forbes*, "The technique produced strong emotional bonds between donor and child, and helped build SCF into a charity with one of the most loyal and committed groups of sponsors in the country."[1]

Since SCF's founding in 1932, their ads had featured prominent photos of appealing waifs and copy pleading with readers to "adopt" a child by mail. But as time went on, SCF realized it could make much better use of its funds by sponsoring community development programs that helped hundreds of children and adults at the same time.

As the *Forbes* articles points out, SCF changed its ads to pitches for community development projects. This made sense, since the last direct check mailed to a child had been sent in 1984. But the ads bombed. Why? People simply aren't motivated by community projects the way they are by pathetic-looking waifs. Community projects are vague, ill defined, and not easily visualized or dramatized. A starving child, on the other hand, is a specific, vivid, gut-wrenching, pitiable object with whom readers can identify immediately.

It doesn't matter that using money to help one child at a time is not nearly as efficient as helping batches of kids and adults together; people are more likely to send money if they are promised *the immediate gratification of a personalized, emotional payoff.*

The lesson is clear: The more immediate, specific, vivid and personal you allow your agency to make the emotional payoff in your advertising, the more effective it is likely to be.

## TO BECOME A BETTER JUDGE OF ADVERTISING COPY, GET IN THE HABIT OF CAREFULLY STUDYING SHORT PIECES OF SUPERB WRITING

It is not difficult. If you don't live in Los Angeles or New York City, have the *Los Angeles Times* or *The New York Times* sent to you daily. Read *The Wall Street Journal*. Read Jane Brody's health column in the *New York Times*. Read Russell Baker's column or, better yet, his wonderful memoir, *Growing Up*.

Reporters and columnists for major newspapers are expert at writing against a deadline, for a literate but impatient audience. They know how to make complicated things easy to understand without oversimplifying them. Jane Brody, for example, writes with great clarity about complex, controversial, very technical subjects.

With some exceptions, I don't recommend fiction. Commercial fiction is written solely to entertain, and has nothing to do with advertising. And serious fiction clearly is of a much higher order than ads and newspaper columns. It uses much more complex techniques because it has a far more profound and complex purpose. Also, the length of even the shortest of short stories is limited only by its author's imagination. Ads are limited by far stricter demands of time, space, and production schedules.

On the other hand, there are certain works of fiction that ad managers may find helpful because they demonstrate so powerfully that in prose of any kind, less is often more. Two excellent examples are the Ernest Hemingway short stories "A Clean, Well-Lighted Place" and "The Killers." Both have been reprinted in *Ernest Hemingway: The Snows of Kilimanjaro and Other Stories* (Collier Books/Macmillan Publishing Company).

## "STIX NIX HICK PIX"

That was *Variety*'s headline to indicate that cornball movies about farmers were unpopular with rural folk. The headline was terse, vivid, and colorful—it attracted people's attention, amused them, and informed them all at once. It's a terrific example of lively writing. Try to make the copy in your advertising equally lively.

Generally speaking, copy should be written to sound the way people talk. People use short words when they talk, especially when they want to impress other people or when they want to convey emotion, as they do when they're feeling happy, angry, or sexually aroused. Long words and long, flowing sentences tend to interfere with emotion because they call attention to themselves. As a rule, the words in ads that paint the most vivid pictures are short words.

## THE COPY IN YOUR ADS IS PROBABLY TOO LONG

In *Management in Small Doses*, Russel L. Ackoff of the University of Pennsylvania's Wharton School points out that not only do managers have far too much to read, but also, the more they feel pressured to read, the less they actually do read.

Ackoff and his colleagues performed an experiment in which two groups of four scientific papers, one above average and one below, were heavily edited. Each group contained one complete paper, one reduced by one-third, the next by two-thirds, and the fourth by 95 percent. The results showed no significant difference in comprehension for the above-average reports even when they were reduced to only one-third their original length. The same was true of the below-average reports, with one exception. Those who had read only the abstract—the report that had been reduced to only 5 percent of its original length—actually obtained a *higher* score!

Ackoff's conclusion: "even good scientific writing could be reduced by at least two-thirds without much loss of content." Obviously, the shorter a piece of bad writing is, the more people are likely to get out of it—or, in Ackoff's words, "the optimal length of a bad message is zero."[2]

After twenty-three years of commercial writing of all kinds, including speeches, books, essays, columns, feature articles, radio and TV commercials, and print ads, I am convinced that most written pieces are too long. Almost all print ads are too long. Most books and articles are too long. If even good scientific writing, which one would expect to be packed with facts, can be reduced by two-thirds with no loss of comprehension—and the comprehension of bad writing whose length is reduced by 95 percent actually improves—can you imagine what would happen if you cut the copy in most print ads by at least half? And what about the viewer bombarded by hundreds of commercials in the average evening? I would bet that if the copy in those commercials was cut to a fifty-word average, comprehension of copy points would rise.

## HOW COPY SHOULD BE STRUCTURED

Generally speaking, printed copy can be divided into three not necessarily equal parts. The first part, which is usually relatively short, makes the transition between the headline and the copy block, and introduces the second section. The second section goes into detail. The final section wraps things up. Usually the last paragraph ends with a clever signoff that refers back to some of the wording or phrasing used in the headline.

## A MNEMONIC CAN WORK QUITE WELL, BUT IT CAN BE CORNY

A mnemonic is any device that aids memory. In commercials it usually involves a figure of speech or a phrase that is literally depicted. For example, a newspaper that claims to "enlighten" its readers will be shown lighting up a reader's face as she opens its pages.

A campaign for Tropicana orange juice used a very effective mnemonic. It showed shadows of palm trees like those seen in Florida creeping over scenes that were clearly not shot in Florida. Those shadows, evoking the tropics, vividly connoted "fresh orange juice."

Mnemonics can help make a selling premise come alive on TV, but they can be offputting to viewers if they are too blatant or obvious, or if they seem simpleminded.

## HOW TO MAKE BETTER HEADLINES

"How to" headlines can often be shortened, with no loss of impact, by eliminating the phrase "how to." The same thing applies to the word *announcing*. In the 1920s when big-budget advertising was in its infancy, long "how to" headlines worked quite well because readers were used to long newspaper articles and magazine feature stories. Also, a relatively naive, patient populace, newly introduced to middle-class living and eager to take advantage of the flood of new inventions, was willing to wade through paragraph after paragraph of instructive copy. Today's audience is better educated, less patient, and far more sophisticated in a visual sense.

Try to avoid using the ellipsis (three dots) in headlines to create drama or signify a pause or the passage of time. It is a dated, cumbersome device that tends to distract impatient readers and slow down communication.

Headlines written in script are hard to read. Even more than the ellipsis, they distract the reader by calling attention to the physical appearance of the words and interrupting a thought process that should occur in split seconds. Many small advertisers who don't know any better think script conveys a sense of elegance and class. To a minor degree it does, but it is always better to try to communicate prestige and snobbishness by using precisely the right phrasing and verbal texture than by changing the physical appearance of the words. The headlines in BMW ads are an excellent example.

The same goes for headlines on a slant or headlines that are physically separated into two or three separate lines located at different points in an ad.

These suggestions may sound suspiciously like the dreaded "rules" I referred to in an earlier chapter. They are not. They represent the expression of a point of view that is, or should be, self-evident to well-trained copywriters—and to every sophisticated advertiser.

## DON'T CRIPPLE YOUR PRINT BY USING IT TO APE YOUR TV

There's a limit to how much action you can suggest in a still picture. When you try to simulate electronic TV techniques on the page by using trick photography, you don't enhance print's power, you merely underscore how weakly it duplicates film.

The big advantage print has over TV is that readers can pause to study the printed page and ponder the printed message. They have more control over a print ad a foot or two in front of their eyes than they have over the fleeting images that flit across a TV screen ten feet away. This gives print, good print anyway, a private, intimate quality and, I maintain, a more intrusive aspect than most TV. I don't believe print, as such, is necessarily more credible than TV. However, I do believe there is a different quality, for want of a better term we might call it a more "resonant" quality, to its credibility. That quality suffers when bastardized techniques that attract attention on TV are used in print.

## IF YOU USE A WORD PLAY OR DOUBLE ENTENDRE IN YOUR HEADLINE, DON'T USE THE VISUAL TO ILLUSTRATE ONE OF THE MEANINGS

I have talked about this before, but it's worth repeating because this mistake is made literally thousands of times a day by agencies, especially small agencies, and clients who regard the practice as "creative."

The visual must take off from, or amplify the headline. Literally visualizing a pun or word play slows things down and confuses readers by doing some of the work for them that they unconsciously expect to do for themselves. If they pause to dope out a clever bit of word play for themselves, and are amused by it, they are likely to read at least some of your ad. In effect, using the visual to illustrate one of the headline's meanings shuts readers out by doing some of their work for them.

Let's use one of the examples I referred to earlier. Assume you have a headline for your bank that says. "We Put Money In A Whole New Light." A visual that shows a pile of money with a spotlight on it doesn't add anything to the meaning of the headline. It doesn't begin to get at the *reason* that your bank puts money in a whole new light. What this headline is really all about is the fact that your bank offers customers a whole new perspective on the care and handling of money, and that this perspective results in certain actions or procedures, or certain behavior, that benefits the bank's customers. What the bank offers has nothing to do, literally, with lights or piles of money. It has to do with a state of mind, so that's what the visual should refer to. If you can't find an appropriate visual, make do with an all-copy ad. It is the art director's job to make that ad look dramatic and inviting to read. In this particular case, you may need both a new headline and a new visual.

One more example: Let's say your Widget Company produces an in-home pregnancy test kit, and you want to announce that to the world. Your agency writes a clever headline: "Widget Predicts The Present." (In other words, instead of being able to predict *the future*, the customer can tell *right now*, in *the present*, whether or not she's pregnant.) Your first impulse might be to illustrate that headline with some sort of crystal ball. If you really get carried away, you might even consider putting the company logo on the crystal ball. But you'd only be illustrating the headline, not amplifying or adding to it. No more information or drama is added to the ad if you use a photograph of a crystal ball. The trick would be to lay out the ad using your company logo in an interesting way, or illustrating the device, using a close-up shot in limbo.

Sometimes the only thing a strong headline needs is a conventional picture or a bit of visual decoration, a picture, in other words, that doesn't necessarily add anything conceptually, but enhances communication because it makes the ad more attractive to the eye. There's nothing wrong with that. Many of the best ads for foreign cars feature an extremely provocative headline below a simple photograph of the car.

By the way, while we're on the subject—as a rule, the more the picture explains, the less the headline has to, and vice versa.

## QUOTES IN HEADLINES TEND TO BE DULL IN PRINT

The right person talking to the TV camera in the right way can be fascinating. But a picture of that person with a statement from him printed above or below his picture and surrounded by quote marks seems flat, much as a speech does when you read it instead of hearing it delivered. It is much more interesting to create a headline that says something provocative about the person in the picture and put his quote in the copy. The headline can flag the reader by telling him why the person in the picture is somebody important enough to listen to.

Of course, if the person is so famous that his image is immediately recognizable, and if the quote is truly astonishing, that is a different matter. But most of the ads I've seen that use people's pictures and their quotes in the headlines feature company presidents, employees, or customers making bland, generally complimentary statements of interest to few people besides those who paid for the ad.

Quotes are usually more effective if they are *not* accompanied by a picture of the person making the quote. A quoted headline about a resort, for example, without the person quoted but with a picture of the resort or of one of the resort's features, can be quite effective.

## YOU HAVE VERY LITTLE TO GAIN FROM PRETTY PICTURES THAT ARE NOT GERMANE

I am constantly amazed at the number of ads showing the company chairman or one of its products in front of a background that has nothing to do with the subject of the picture or the ad. It's as though the ad manager has had an inspiration: "Hey, the president looks O.K., but his office looks dull. How about we jazz the shot up a bit by putting a beautiful sunset over Monument Valley behind him?" If the sunset has nothing to do with the president or the reason he's in the ad, it shouldn't be there.

## BREAK UP LONG BLOCKS OF COPY WITH SUBHEADS

Subheads make long copy seem shorter, less intimidating, and easier to read. And cleverly worded subheads make copy seem livelier.

## NOT ALL ADS NEED TAG LINES

Tag lines, like musical themes, can sum up your message succinctly and cleverly, help position your product, and help your campaign come to life. Three excellent examples that come to mind are "BMW/The Ultimate Driving Machine," "The American Express Card/Don't Leave Home Without It," and "It Takes A Tough Man To Make A Tender Chicken" (Perdue chicken).

A tag line is not a description. It can be thought of as a stirring or clever summing up of what the product is or what it does.

On the other hand, a tag line inserted into a campaign just for the sake of having one can prove burdensome. Tag lines take up valuable space and time in print ads and TV commercials; they must pull their weight. Dull, lackluster tag lines are far worse than no tag line at all.

## DON'T WASTE YOUR TIME
## WITH HEADLINES THAT RHYME

People do not speak in rhyme, so they are put off by the singsong, childish quality of rhyming headlines. Rhyming headlines sound awkward because they seem precious and highly contrived—and any set of words that sounds contrived lacks credibility.

Rhyming headlines can be appropriate under certain circumstances—when your ad or campaign is a parody or take-off, for example, or if you are making a specific point about language or rhyming in general.

## IF YOU FOOL AROUND WITH BEAUTIFUL YOUNG GIRLS
## IN BIKINIS, YOU MAY GET CAUGHT SHORT

Do not put beautiful young women in bikinis in your advertising unless you are selling a product that has some direct relationship to young women, bikinis, or both. A surprising number of advertisers in auto buff books continue to sell auto accessories by prominently displaying pictures of buxom girls in bikinis. It is corny, it is distracting, and it reflects poorly on the manufacturer's taste and the quality of the product. It is difficult for adults to take a product seriously when it is advertised in this way.

## BORROWED INTEREST

You use borrowed interest when you try to "borrow" the interest the reader or viewer has in a subject unrelated to your product or service, and attach that interest to your product. For example: "Just as the fine Eskimo artists you see here work an ivory walrus tusk into beautiful sculptures of whales and seals, Widget Company structural analysts use computer-aided design to create the world's most finely balanced ship propellers."

Some people confuse borrowed interest with any kind of comparison. The difference is, borrowed interest is a *forced* or *labored* or *highly exaggerated* comparison. It is almost always more effective to dramatize something intrinsic to your product than to try to borrow interest. When you borrow, your force the reader to do a lot of work, comparatively speaking, in order to dope out what you're getting at—and when he's all through, you have not given him much of a reward for all that work. Figuring out a bit of clever word play in a headline, on the other hand, rewards him the way a comic's joke or a magician's trick rewards him for his attention; there's a sense of playfulness about the joke or the trick in a clever headline that viewers find stimulating.

## IF YOUR ADVERTISING IS USUALLY APPROVED AT THE LAST MINUTE, FORCING THE ENGRAVER OR YOUR PRODUCTION COMPANY INTO EXPENSIVE OVERTIME, YOUR COMPANY IS DOING SOMETHING WRONG

Rushing creative work often results in errors. It also results in mediocre work. Creative people who must work around the clock and over weekends to get work out on time can never produce the level of quality they are able to when they have the time they need to do the job right. If overtime and late charges are a chronic part of the way your company does business, I would strongly suggest you reorganize your approval process, and perhaps your entire advertising or marketing department, because it's an indication of serious organizational problems.

## DO NOT MAKE THE MISTAKE OF THINKING YOUR AUDIENCE CAN ONLY RELATE TO PEOPLE EXACTLY LIKE THEMSELVES

It usually makes sense to use actors and models whose age, sex, and apparent income mirror your target audience's. You would not, for example, advertise a Lincoln Town Car with an eighteen-year old driver at the wheel alongside his sixteen-year old date. But it pays to allow your agency to cast interesting-looking people—what casting directors call "character" types—in your commercials instead of the usual bland, attractive types most advertisers go for.

If your advertising is provocative, people will be interested in the stories your ads tell, just as they are interested in provocative, well-written plays whether or not the plays are about people exactly like themselves. You don't have to be a salesman or have a father who committed suicide to be moved to tears by the plight of Willy Loman in Arthur Miller's *Death of a Salesman*. And you don't have to be a middle-aged male from the sticks to be amused by the two characters in the Bartles & James wine cooler commercials.

## TOO MANY COOKS WILL SPOIL YOUR BROTH

If I were an advertising czar who had control over every client, I would dictate that someone bring a kitchen timer to every meeting in which advertising was being evaluated. I would set the timer at forty-five minutes and, when the bell rang, I would force all the client reps to stop talking and make a yes or no decision. An ad campaign is not *War and Peace* and a TV campaign is not *Intolerance*. As has been said many times by many an admaker in the privacy of his office after an interminable client meeting, *it's only advertising*. We're trying to sell things to people by using words and pictures. How complicated can that be? How many angels can dance on the head of a pin?

And I would order that no more than three client representatives at the very most could attend any meeting in which creative work was being reviewed for approval. No doubt that sounds unworkable and naive to people who work for large companies. But the idea is not unworkable and it is not naive if the three people involved enjoy the faith and trust of top management, have sufficient guts, thoroughly understand advertising, and enjoy working with adpeople. It only sounds unworkable because almost nobody has done it yet. (I have it on good authority that certain clients do indeed operate this way. Hyundai, whose award-winning advertising has been enormously successful, is one. I have been told that two or three people, and nobody else, approve all their advertising. Miller Brewing Company is another. "There is only one guy there who can kill advertising," a highly placed friend at one of their agencies told me. "Loads of people can look at it, so they can feel they know what's going on. He tells his people, 'You can all see it, but you can't kill it, only *I* can kill it.' It's really great. It makes the agency feel wonderful because we don't have to waste a lot of time and energy fighting to keep great advertising from being ruined.")

## HEADLINES IN PRINT ADS ARE USUALLY PLACED BELOW THE PICTURE. THEY DON'T HAVE TO BE

The picture is usually at the top of an ad and the headline placed directly beneath because that's what most people are used to seeing in newspapers and books, where captions explain pictures.

That doesn't mean headlines can't be at the top of the page, or anywhere else on the page, or that pictures can't be at the bottom or on the right or the left.

Headlines are almost always set much bigger than copy because large type is easier and more inviting to read. However, creative people and clients should feel as free to break that rule as any other. An excellent series of print ads for Amtrak that ran several years ago featured headlines in the same type size as the copy blocks. The headlines were separated from the copy with a large amount of white space—placement that would be anathema to most art directors. Small pictures of various services and benefits train travel offered passengers were indented into the copy blocks. The ads worked very well and won a number of creative awards.

## BEFORE YOU SIGN OFF ON A STORYBOARD, MAKE SURE YOU AND YOUR AGENCY ARE IN AGREEMENT ON EVERY DETAIL OF THAT COMMERCIAL

Just as an architect can look at a blueprint and "see" what the three-dimensional product will look like in his mind's eye, art directors and writers can look at a storyboard and "see" how they want the film to look, in what way and at what pace they want the action and copy to flow, and so forth. Their job is to learn to communicate what they see to the client clearly before he signs production estimates.

The client's job is to learn to see things the way the agency people see them by developing his visual instincts. All differences of opinion must be ironed out before shooting begins. Don't try to be "nice," figuring differences can be ironed out at some later meeting. If you do, you will wind up second guessing your creative people, and that is not good. It frustrates and distracts them and undermines their confidence.

## AT THE RISK OF GIVING YOU A TENSION HEADACHE, I'M GOING TO TALK ABOUT TENSION AGAIN

Tension is such a crucial element in practically every piece of advertising, especially print advertising, and so few clients understand it, that I thought it would be worth discussing a second time.

Many years ago, psychologists performed an experiment in which they put a number of people in a room, alone except for a ring toss set. It was one of those children's toys with a short wooden post held upright on the floor and a bunch of round hemp rings. The subjects were left alone to amuse themselves as best they could. As expected, with time to kill, they began trying to try to toss the rings around the post. What the psychologists discovered was that most of the people moved far enough away from the post so that tossing the rings around it was challenging but not so difficult as to be totally frustrating. In other words, they deliberately positioned themselves between frustration on the one hand and boredom on the other. The process of alternately producing and relieving tension was what made the activity stimulating.

The best advertising is like that; it creates a sense of tension, or drama, by piquing the reader's or viewer's curiosity. It puzzles the reader slightly, or surprises or shocks him.

I wrote earlier about the importance of leaving out a key ingredient in your headline–visual combination in order to pique people's interest. The fact that your headline and your visual are each perfectly clear, but their connection to each other is a bit puzzling because you have left out one ingredient, is what creates a subtle bit of tension in the reader—tension he seeks to relieve by mentally supplying the missing ingredient. The high point of the craft of advertising lies in creating just enough tension to pique his curiosity but not enough to frustrate him so that he turns the page.

When you study print ads, try to learn to distinguish between those whose headline–visual combination creates a bit of tension in the reader and those that don't.

## DON'T BE BOUND BY THE CONSTRICTIONS (OR CONVENTIONS) OF THE TV FRAME

Learn to think in terms that transcend the boundaries of the ordinary TV frame on a storyboard. Today's audiences are sophisticated. They will understand what you're getting at if, for example, the actors in your spots talk to offscreen announcers. Playwrights use the technique of having on-stage actors talk to unseen characters, or directly to the audience. Actors in costume may enter the theater from the back of the auditorium and begin speaking as they walk toward the stage. Actors have entered the theater on horseback and walked through the audience; in the Broadway show *Starlight Express,* actors skated through the audience. Don't be afraid to let actors in your commercials kid the product, or admit they're actors. Dog food makers, once quite conservative sponsors, produce successful, quite sophisticated commercials with talking dogs and singing cats. Even horses can talk on camera, as Mr. Ed proved.

By the way, these techniques, or at least this way of thinking, can be applied to print, too. Some years ago, in its work for Cutty Sark Scotch, Scali, McCabe Sloves created a holiday season billboard painted to make it appear that a big red ribbon had been wrapped around the entire thirty-foot billboard.

## KIDS IN COMMERCIALS: WHEN THEY'RE GOOD, THEY'RE VERY VERY GOOD; WHEN THEY'RE BAD, THEY'RE HORRIBLE

Kids in commercials can be wonderfully charming. There's no substitute for a great child actor. But a kid who is frightened, angry, or tired can bring a whole shoot to a halt. You can help avoid problems by: (1) using an adult actor along with the kid or kids in your commercial; (2) avoiding giving children long, involved stretches of dialogue; (3) making sure your agency hires a production house with a director who is patient and has experience with child actors; (4) having backup kids on hand; (5) refraining from wringing your hands and acting the part of the worried client if you're on the set during the shoot and a kid screws up or blows up or starts to cry; and (6) approving a shooting schedule that allows plenty of time to get the right performance out of the kids. Spending more time and money to get it right in the first place makes a lot more sense than wasting thousands of dollars in sound studios dubbing the kids' voices long after the director has wrapped the shoot.

## DON'T FORCE YOUR AGENCY TO WRITE TWENTY-EIGHT SECONDS OF COPY FOR A THIRTY-SECOND COMMERCIAL

Actors need time to make a scene "play." That is, it takes a certain amount of time to execute the gestures, intonations, pauses, body movements, and facial expressions that actors use to make a scene come alive before the camera. Directors need time to execute certain camera moves, set up certain camera angles, and so forth. The more an actor has to rush through his lines, the less of his talents he's able to bring to bear on his part. The less free time that's written into a script, the less freedom and discretion a director has to plan and execute his shots.

But many advertisers seem convinced the copywriter is wasting valuable time if his TV commercial script can be read in anything less than twenty-nine and a half seconds. Usually, rather than antagonize an obdurate client, the agency leaves it to the director to tell the client that the script simply cannot be performed and shot without being substantially trimmed. Sometimes the script is rewritten by the client on the set, and shooting is constantly interrupted as the client dashes off to get the approval of each new scribble by senior management. All this could be avoided if the ad and marketing executives understood more about writing plays and acting in them. Or if senior management trusted their agency enough to abide by what they told them about script length in the first place.

## BE PREPARED TO TAKE SOME RISKS TO AVOID BLANDNESS. AIM FOR ADVERTISING THAT PERSONALIZES YOUR CORPORATION

To advertise is to take risks; risk-averse executives make lousy advertising managers. To communicate effectively and move people emotionally, an ad, like a play or novel, must have a point of view; it must come at the reader from point A or point B or point C.

An ad's point of view is its backbone—to the degree that it has one, it may irritate or confuse some consumers. Trying to produce advertising that appeals equally to everyone results in bland advertising.

You have to accept the fact, and not worry about it, that a significant percentage of your potential audience is unreachable. Filling your advertising with copy points and benefits and pictures of your product in use and guarantees and boasts and claims will not attract these people's attention. What it *will* do is prevent the ads from reaching the people whose lives you might conceivably touch if your advertising was bolder, simpler and more single-minded.

The more bureaucratic your corporation is, the less charming, interesting, memorable, and provocative your advertising is likely to be. A corporation protected from consumers by layer upon layer of risk-averse committees who must pass on every piece of advertising is likely to seem aloof and distant to consumers, and its advertising sterile and flat.

*Wall Street Journal* staff reporter Larry Reibstein wrote an interesting article about corporate speech writers that is apropos:

Accessibility and willingness to reveal a personal side are why speakers like [Lee] Iacocca are so successful, [but] many writers complain that they seldom get to tailor their work to an executive's personality or speaking style because they are denied access to him. That helps to explain why so many corporate speeches sound depressingly alike and tell the audience little about the speaker. . . . For nearly every corporate speech, writers say, editing battles are fought over managers' tendency to inject lots of numbers and technical jargon . . . drafts of even minor speeches are routinely channeled through numerous bureaucratic levels, with unsurprising results. . . . "We can't say that; we don't want to imply this. Let's not get anyone angry at us." Everyone, to be seen as doing their [sic] job, has to do something to the speech . . . you end up with vanilla pudding."[3]

## A FOOLISH CONSISTENCY, EMERSON SAID, IS THE HOBGOBLIN OF LITTLE MINDS. BUT AN INTELLIGENT CONSISTENCY IS THE KEY TO EFFECTIVE ADVERTISING.

If your advertising is working, resist the impulse to change it. You will tire of it long before the public does. If something goes wrong at your ad agency, resist the impulse to change agencies. Sophisticated advertisers stay with their agencies a long time. Fickle advertisers, who know very little about advertising and don't trust agencies, change agencies frequently.

## ALWAYS COMPLIMENT YOUR AGENCY

When you evaluate work, make sure the agency people know you appreciate how hard they've worked and how much thought they've put into the advertising they show you. I know it's their job. And they know you know it's their job. The point is, creative people invest a good deal of themselves in their work, and they appreciate being applauded for their efforts whether or not you think their work will prove to be effective.

Whenever possible, try to react noticeably and positively when the creative people first show you advertising. Nothing is worse than showing work to a bunch of frozen faces. If you have problems with the work, withhold your criticisms for a few minutes, until all the work has been shown and you have had time to say a few complimentary words about the entire presentation.

## DON'T LET YOURSELF TURN INTO ONE OF THOSE CLIENTS WHO KILLS WITH KINDNESS

Many otherwise decent and humane individuals don't know how to kill advertising they don't like, or like but think won't work. Rather than hurt the agency's feelings, they dillydally, dragging their feet for weeks and leading the agency to believe it's on the verge of a sale.

Don't be like that—it's demoralizing to the agency. Tell your agency firmly but diplomatically that the advertising they've created is not for you. Explain why in as much detail as you can. If you can, give them suggestions for other ways to go, with which you might be more comfortable. Don't be defensive. Don't bully your account executive. Don't lecture. Don't blame your senior management. Face the problem squarely, accept the responsibility for your personal preferences, deal with them, and get on with it. Handling your agency in this way is better for their morale and yours. In the long run, good morale means better advertising.

## IF YOU'RE UNSURE WHETHER OR NOT TO APPROVE A PIECE OF ADVERTISING, DON'T SOLICIT THE OPINIONS OF A BUNCH OF SECRETARIES IN YOUR OFFICE

The prime reason creative people choose a given headline–visual combination is to attract attention in a meaningful, believable, relevant way. If you've already gotten your secretaries' attention by thrusting an ad under their noses, you've bypassed the first important test of a good ad. Also, it's intimidating to be asked to make an off-the-top-of-the-head public judgment about your employer's advertising. The benefits you derive from such "research" are likely to be equal to its cost—zero.

## WHAT TO DO WHEN YOU THINK YOUR ADVERTISING
## MAY BE GETTING AWAY FROM YOU

An eccentric but clever art director I worked with many years ago let me in on the sugar solution. His name was Shelly. "You know what sugar is, right?" Shelly asked me aggressively soon after we had started working together.

You know what it does, right? But sometimes you get so bollixed up trying to solve a problem all the nutcase client types and research bimbos and suits [account executives] have made complicated, you find yourself going off the deep end. They will have started to slice the baloney so thin that you can't even taste it, you know what I mean? That's when you got to force yourself to go back to the basics. You got to remind yourself there's a bunch of guys way over there on the left side saying, "If we make such and such a product that does such and such for people, those people way over there on the right side might actually buy it." And you are one of the adguys, stuck right in the middle. It's up to you to tell the people way over on the right side, the consumers, just what it is the guys on the left got for 'em, in a way they will pay attention to and understand.

Advertising's as simple as that, when you get right down to it. If you're advertising sugar, you don't run to the research guys and do focus groups and divide people up into artificial groups by age and income or anything like that. First, you sit down on your own backside, with your own self, and you ask yourself, "Self, what is sugar?" And every time you get away from the simple facts of what sugar is and what it does that people want, you bring yourself back to the basics. Believe me, it sounds a lot simpler and easier than it is!

To some extent, we are all victims of the machinery invented to serve us. High-tech electronics, computers, spreadsheets, jargon, production experts, music experts, word experts, media experts, research experts, fancy lunches, and focus groups have a way of overwhelming plain old common sense—especially when large amounts of money are involved.

When you're not certain that your advertising really says what you want it to say, and you've got a sneaky private feeling a mindless juggernaut has been set in motion that will wind up dragging you to your destruction by your ankles, here's what you should do: Lock your office door, disconnect your office phone, turn off your PC, and—on a legal pad, in pencil—write down, "What is sugar?" And under that headline, write down, as simply as possible, what kind of product it is that you are selling, and what it offers people. Write, "I should buy this product because . . . " and see if you can finish the statement in no more than twelve or fifteen words. Spread all your print ads on your desk or conference table and see if they answer the question in a way most reasonably intelligent people would accept. Run a tape of your commercials or study your storyboards, and demand the same thing of them.

Shelly was right. What is very basic is not always very easy. But it can be very, very helpful.

## HOW TO AVOID THE DANGERS THAT COME WITH INCREDIBLE SUCCESS

No matter how many years of experience they have, the pros in Hollywood and on and off Broadway still can't predict which movies and shows will be stupendous hits and which won't.

To some extent, the same is true of advertising agencies. From a creative point of view, the scope of the job agencies are called on to do is quite limited, so the quality of their output is far more predictable. But the essence of phenomenal success is still both unpredictable and unanalyzable. At times, an agency hits paydirt and its client enjoys a bonanza—the client's slogan ("Where's the beef?" or "We make money the old fashioned way—we earn it") is on everybody's lips. Johnny Carson jokes about it, *People* magazine writes about it. Awareness soars, sales skyrocket, and everybody congratulates himself on his own brilliance.

When this happens, it's great, and agencies are inclined to act as though it was inevitable, given their creative genius. Clients like to think they had a big part in it, too. The problem comes when the agency's next effort is merely superlative and effective and wonderful—but not stupendous. Where, the chairman asks, are the comedians who repeat our tag line on national TV? Why aren't people stenciling it on T-shirts?

Andy Warhol once said that everybody in America would be famous for ten minutes. That would be great if it happened, but you shouldn't blame your agency if, having pulled it off once, they can't pull it off twice. Something in the nature of creativity makes a certain amount of unevenness inevitable. Beethoven wrote "Wellington's Victory," Mozart wrote some boring sonatas, and Hemingway wrote *To Have and Have Not*. If you and your agency do hit a nationwide home run the first time at bat, try to resist the impulse to believe your own press clippings. It'll make it a lot easier to accept the jeers and brickbats when you only hit a single, or, God help you, strike out the next couple of times you come to the plate.

## THERE IS NO SUCH THING AS A SIMPLE OR UNCOMPLICATED SHOOT

Shooting commercials is never easy. There are always unexpected problems, missed opportunities, necessary shortcuts, and so forth. Even on simple, 16mm or tape shoots of fifteen-second commercials in a studio, the pressure is enormous. Anything that helps lessen the pressure helps the shoot, and anything that heightens the pressure hinders the shoot.

Always try to give your agency the time they need to pick the TV commercial director they want. Losing their favorite director because his bid is too high is something all agencies learn to live with. If they can't live with it, there are informal ways they can get the person they want. But if your company waits so long to approve a commercial that the agency must settle for bidding it to the directors who are still available rather than to those they want, chances are the work will suffer.

What's more, the magic that can happen when actors are in the hands of top creative and production people almost never happens when the director and the ad agency people are not completely simpatico. So do everything you can to keep the pressure off and help the magic happen by approving storyboards early.

# SEVEN QUESTIONS EVERY ADVERTISER WOULD LIKE HIS AGENCY TO ANSWER, BUT IS TOO EMBARRASSED TO ASK

## 15

**Q:** I know there is a lot of personnel turnover in agencies. Doesn't this affect the work they can do for clients? And is there any way I can keep turnover from having a damaging effect on my account?

**A:** High turnover rates don't seem to affect the quality of the work agencies do for clients. Agencies known for mediocre work continue to do mediocre work no matter how many highly talented people they attract, and good agencies continue to do good work no matter how many good people they lose.

If the handful of people who own and control the agency have the guts, brains, talent, and determination to fight for good work, good work will result. If they are determined to make as much money as they can as fast as they can by giving all their clients whatever kind of creative work appears to make the client happy, the result will be mediocre work. Think of it this way: The *New York Times* loses part of its staff every year, but it continues to produce a high-quality newspaper. Even if the turnover rates increased to 20 percent or more a year, The *Times* would still remain the *Times. The National Enquirer*, on the other hand, would remain the *Enquirer* even if they hired the top fifty graduates of the nation's best journalism schools every year for the next ten years. A creative business organization remains the kind of organization it is in spite of staff changes because the people who own and run it have a certain perspective about the kind of values they want the organization to represent.

On the other hand, advertising agencies, like businesses of any kind, change as time goes on. "Hot" agencies do not stay hot forever—at least not as hot as they once were. As yesterday's hot agencies grow bigger, newer, hotter agencies take their place. Professionals who work with numbers are familiar with the phrase "regression to the mean." It means that as time goes on, the accumulated results of any action or series of actions begin to cluster more and more toward the average. Short parents tend to have taller children, tall parents have shorter children, and so forth.

Agencies change in the same way, and probably at more or less the same pace, that clients do. Clients who maintain close, trusting relationships with their agencies, based on mutual tolerance and respect, do not have to worry very much about turnover. They will wind up with the best work possible no matter who is on their account, because the morale of the agency people on their account will be high. By the same token, clients who change agencies frequently and treat their agencies as supplicants don't have to worry about turnover, either. Regardless of whether agency turnover is high or low, they will not get anything like the best work possible because the morale of the people working on their account will be low.

**Q:** I'll tell you frankly, some of my advertising executives, maybe more than some, give our agencies a tough time because they resent the big salaries agency people make. How much *do* they make?

**A:** Judged by the standards of most white-collar professional or semiprofessional college graduates, I'm not sure agency account executives and creative people make all that much. A few years ago I did a private, confidential, and informal survey of agency salaries. I spoke at length, in confidence, with my accountant, Jerry Kindman. His firm handles the tax returns of over four thousand advertising professionals. I also spoke at length with half a dozen of the top placement people in the business. I compared what they told me with figures provided by a number of personnel executives at the top New York agencies.

The figures are for the larger agencies (say, $25 million in billings and up) in New York City. Out-of-town salaries tend to be lower, especially for smaller agencies, but they have been creeping up rapidly during the last five years. Branches of large New York agencies pay what the home offices pay.

Basically, salaries fall between the fast trackers on the high side and the slow trackers on the low side. Kindman's figures were generally slightly lower than those the placement people provided. To provide a reasonable variation, I have combined Kindman's lowest figure with the placement people's highest in each category. The original figures were for 1984. I asked Jerry Kindman if he would have his staff spend a few minutes updating the figures to 1988.

For a writer or art director: beginner, $15,000 to $25,000; one to two years experience, $20,000 to $30,000; three to four years, $25,000 to $40,000; five to seven years, $30,000 to $60,000; seven to ten years, $40,000 to $75,000; ten to fifteen years, $45,000 to $90,000; fifteen to twenty-five years, $55,000 to $250,000.

For an account executive: beginner, $20,000 to $25,000; one to two years experience, $20,000 to $30,000; three to four years, $25,000 to $40,000; five to seven years, $30,000 to $50,000; seven to ten years, $40,000 to $65,000; ten to fifteen years, $50,000 plus; fifteen to twenty-five years, $60,000 to $250,000.

Placement people usually refuse to give a top figure for account executives who have been in the business more than ten years because many either open their own shops or become part of senior management of large agencies. When that happens, stock, stock options, and other perks make comparative salary estimates meaningless. Of course, the same applies to creative people who rise to the point where they own their own shops or hold large blocks of stock. Generally speaking, the pluggers look to profit sharing to provide them with enough to support them after retirement, while fast-trackers are more interested in stock. Most people reach a plateau from which their salary rises slowly. The average, talented, experienced, middle-aged professional in a reasonably large New York shop levels off, at this writing, in the neighborhood of $75,000 to $110,000. He can still expect salary increases, but usually his income will edge up, not jump. In addition, most shops offer some sort of profit sharing and stock purchase plan. Profit sharing at a well-run agency usually runs from 10 to 15 percent of a person's annual salary.

**Q:** I'd like to give my account to a "boutiquey" agency, but I've always had the idea they give research short shrift because they feel it hampers their creative people. That seems short-sighted to me.

**A:** The day of the boutique is over. The hottest of the small, hot shops of the 1970s and early 1980s don't exist anymore. Just about all the famous and successful ones—Carl Ally, Scali, McCabe, Sloves, Lord Geller Federico, Jerry Della Femina & Partners, Ammirati & Puris, Levine, Huntley Schmidt & Beaver, and a number of other highly creative shops—are now highly creative, full-service, powerhouse divisions of large agencies.

I have always felt *boutique* was a misleading term, anyway. It implies preciousness, creativity for its own sake, and a disregard of marketing and research. That may have been true of some two- and three-person shops that opened up in the 1960s and 1970s—and closed a few years later. But all the highly talented creative people I have known or worked for, including the stars who have made a name for themselves in the past twenty years, were very disciplined people who had great respect for both marketing and research. Even when these people's shops were very small, before they could afford to have complete service departments of their own, they made extensive use of independent marketing and research facilities. Some of the stars' penchant and talent for publicity and their flair for promotion overshadowed their instinctive marketing and research talents. Since marketing and research do not lend themselves to provocative statements that newspapers, magazines, and TV stations pick up, many advertisers got the idea that well-known creative stars were only interested in creativity for its own sake.

If you like the creative work a certain agency does, and you think your company would benefit from creative work with similar spark and flair, hire them. Rest assured they have as much respect for research as you do, and will recommend its use whenever they feel it's necessary.

**Q:** Why does it take agencies so long to come up with creative work?

**A:** In too many cases, anxious account executives mislead clients by promising them they will be able to see new creative work in practically no time, because they think the client will interpret that as "good service." It is anything but good service; it is, in fact, accommodation to the point of prostitution.

Generally speaking, a large volume of high-caliber creative work cannot be churned out simply by placing a given number of highly paid art and copy monkeys in front of a given number of word processors and drawing boards and working them day and night and on weekends until the advertising equivalent of *Hamlet* emerges. Work created by that sort of system (which is prevalent in certain very large agencies and is an ever-present danger in all large agencies) is almost always devoid of any spark of wit or spontaneity. The exhausting, desperate, plodding nature of this factory-like routine filters any hint of charm or subtlety or grace, and certainly any touch of genuine individuality, out of the final product. Oddly, the creative managers of this sort of nightmare usually wind up very proud of their creative judgment. They mistake riding herd on a mass of overworked, harassed individuals for "leadership," and when the dust has settled they congratulate themselves not so much for choosing the right work—more often than not, the right amalgam of several disparate pieces of work—but for being able to make the "right" decision despite their exhaustion.

Admittedly, some agencies are lazy, some are understaffed, and some are badly managed. All of that can contribute to delays in getting creative work out on time. But the fact is, good creative work takes time, and great creative work takes even longer.

Why does it take so long? By way of an answer, allow me a momentary digression. After I was graduated from college, I served a couple of years as a gunnery officer in the U.S. Navy, standing underway watches on the bridge of the heavy cruiser *U.S.S. Los Angeles*. I learned that at night you can rarely see a set of lights at or near the horizon by staring at a given spot. You must sweep the horizon slowly with your binoculars. For some unexplained reason, your brain will pick up a passing or moving bit of light that interrupts the blackness, but will blind itself to that same bit of light if you simply stare at the point where you think you might have seen it.

The same thing applies to coming up with creative solutions to advertising problems. If you run at the problem head on, like a bull charging a matador, you may miss the solution that will appear as soon as you adopt an oblique point of view. For the creative person, the solution is to keep his mind in motion as he attacks the problem. That may mean sitting alone at the typewriter or drawing board and writing down every line or phrase or thought or situation that comes into his head. It may mean hours of talk between writer and art director, each in turn suggesting visuals and headlines to the other. It may mean wandering down to the canteen for a cup of coffee, or taking a walk around the block.

Some people take breaks continually as they work. To an outsider, it looks as though the writer and art director are sitting around shooting the breeze. Their feet are up on their desks. They laugh, tell jokes and stories, and appear to take nothing very seriously. They swap dirty stories, talk about cars or money or women (if they're men) or men (if they're women) or sports or clothes or restaurants. They discuss books, religion, politics, their families, TV shows, movies, plays. But suddenly, in mid-sentence, one person will say to the other "How about this for a headline?" Or, "What about a visual of . . . ?" And they're off and running, creatively speaking. Feeling they're on a roll, they will work very intensely for perhaps twenty minutes. Then one will say, "Nah, that headline, it just doesn't sit right, y'know? I mean the tonality is off a hair, it's just not quite right." The other person will counter with, "A lot you know, I happen to love it," but without letting his partner know, he'll pick up his pad and draw a line through the headline or the idea for the commercial. Then the idle chatter will start again.

The reason the process seems to work in this bumbling, slow, clumsy way is that part of the art director's or writer's unconscious mind, or "day brain," concentrates on what he sees and does, while another part, the "night brain," concentrates on the creative problem. In effect, he's "sweeping the horizon," looking for clues to the creative solution that represents that "telltale flash of light" we naval officers used to look for in our binoculars. Often this sweeping appears recreational; that's why, in contrast to the staid, stolid, hushed atmosphere in the account services department, there appears to be so much laughter and horseplay in agency creative departments.

This day brain–night brain business does not work very well when the writer is running to catch a train or attending a meeting or writing a report or a memo. Conducting successful horizon searches requires a person to feel safe and relaxed. Emotional confrontations can throw a creative person off, sometimes for hours. Sometimes, even if the atmosphere in the office is pleasant, after a number of hours it may inhibit an individual's creative impulses. He may simply need a change of location to get his brain in gear again.

Most creative work looks terrific when it's fresh from the oven. But great writing, it has been said more than once, lies in rewriting. And rewriting takes time.

The creative managers at agencies with "hot" creative reputations are extremely demanding, which means it usually takes their staffs a long time to satisfy them. That, in turn, means their clients must learn to be patient. On more than one occasion when I worked for Ed McCabe, in the early 1970s, he did what few if any other bosses in my experience have had the nerve to do—he killed work after it had been approved by the client because he had decided it was not up to snuff.

Many creative directors are never quite satisfied that their work is as perfect as it could be. Even after mechanicals have been made, they continue to noodle copy. And they do not hesitate to make copy changes while they're recording radio spots or shooting commercials. Of course, they cannot operate this way unless they feel their clients have complete confidence in their creative judgment. A large component of confidence is patience.

**Q:** In spite of everything you've said about what constitutes good and bad advertising, my experience with agencies leads me to believe that judging ads is 99 percent subjective.

**A:** I don't agree. I am convinced there are certain standards of excellence, in terms of what is and is not provocative, that most of the best senior creative people in the advertising community agree on.

I have kept close watch on the results of the top award shows—The One Show, the Art Directors Club, and the Andy contest—for more than twenty years, and

I have taken part in many judgings. I can tell you that, year after year, there is surprising unanimity in the judgments.

Private judgments of creative talent and achievement are expressed quite baldly and openly in the New York job market. Creative people with certain kinds of portfolios, from certain kinds of agencies, generally have first crack at the most promising jobs and the biggest salaries. This is perhaps the truest test of what is and is not provocative TV and print advertising, because agency management is laying its money and future on the line when it hires new talent. Broadly speaking, the people who win the most awards in the top creative competitions and the people with the most marketable (and therefore the theoretical "best") portfolios tend to be the same people. Since these people are then in a position to do still more promising work, their success tends to perpetuate itself. These individuals are generally acknowledged by headhunters and agency creative personnel recruiters to be the most talented, or the most marketable, or whatever other adjective you want to use to describe them. Career-wise, they can pretty much call their own shots. Probably fewer than than one percent, probably one-half or one-quarter of 1 percent of the working creative people in New York fall into this category. If judgments of creative merit were 99 percent arbitrary, it seems to be that no circle of stars or semistars or hotshots could or would exist, especially in the highly competitive New York market.

There is one more arena where judgments are made, which unfortunately is closed to clients. When most big agencies pitch large pieces of new business, a number of creative teams are given the same problem and the same information, and are invited to have a crack at solving it. Usually, each team is invited into a large conference room to show their work to the others and to top management. These occasions are among the few where top professionals compete on more or less completely equal terms.

Each team usually favors its own work, of course. Even so, when a team comes up with outstanding advertising, the others in the room always recognize and appreciate it. A murmur will go around the room, people will nod or smile, occasionally some will even applaud briefly. The freshest and most innovative work often does not get shown to the client, for reasons that have more to do with the strategy and tactics of agency pitches and politics than with creative criteria. But the people in any creative department always know exactly which of their peers routinely does the best work—and, in my experience, the judgments are almost always unanimous.

**Q:** My intuitive feeling is that the *fact* of advertising, especially a very large amount of advertising, is often more important than what the advertising says and the way it says it—so it doesn't really matter which agency a client, especially a large client, chooses.

**A:** I can't accept that premise as it's stated, but I do believe there is some truth in it. A great deal of advertising, especially big-budget TV advertising is created not so much to try to convince anybody of anything specific as to create and maintain a presence for the company and its product in the public mind.

In other words, the advertising is basically defensive in nature; it is there because competitive advertising is there. The weight and frequency of the advertising must be roughly equal to the competition's advertising in order to make the cut. If it isn't equal in weight, it must be so frequent, so lavish, so obviously exuberant and expensive, that it at least appears to be in the same ballpark.

That said, I still think the way any piece of advertising says what it says is of vital importance. The implicit communication inherent in a series of fine ad campaigns, run over a period of years, is invaluable. Remember—the best advertising makes long-lasting friends for the brand as well as sales. Remember the old IBM print campaign, "Think"? By identifying IBM with cerebration, it helped put IBM on the map and, in the public mind, identified the company with intellectualism, integrity, tastefulness, and honesty. Without using the words *class* or *brains* or *good taste*, it helped establish IBM as a classy company.

**Q:** All your talk about Chaplin and Ernest Dichter and *Death of a Salesman* is interesting. But in the main, advertising involves appeals to mass markets. Look at the most popular movies and best-selling books. The taste level to which they appeal is abysmally low. Isn't your whole approach to advertising a bit elitist?

**A:** I grant you that when it comes to mass entertainment, public taste is often appalling. But when it comes to selling, we're on an entirely different plane. Commercial entertainment deals with wide-ranging stories that involve physical risk, adventure, sex, and graphic depictions of violent confrontations.

Advertising is much narrower in scope; it deals mostly with mundane ways to solve simple problems. And whereas a TV show or movie must seek to capture the public's attention for sixty or ninety minutes, an ad demands only a couple of seconds of people's time. So, in terms of time, scope, dimension, and depth, the public's level of taste doesn't effect the ad process very much. The things I have been recommending, and which I maintain most advertising lacks in sufficient degree—simplicity, contrast, drama, and freshness—appeal to everyone, regardless of the individual's socioeconomic level or aesthetic predilections.

I don't believe that advertisers need to appeal to the lowest common denominator in order to be successful with the masses. Millions of people, especially young people whose sensibilities have not fully matured, may have an appetite for the kind of entertainment you and I find offensive. But millions of children and adults are sold by innovative, interesting advertising that breaks new ground, and more millions have been entertained by first-rate performers performing in first-rate shows of all kinds. "The Bill Cosby Show," Walter Cronkite, Jackie Mason, Mort Sahl, David Letterman, Huntley and Brinkley, "60 Minutes," "All in the Family," "Hill Street Blues," "The Honeymooners," "Taxi," Jack Benny, Bruce Springsteen, the Beatles, Johnny Carson, Ted Koppel, and Edward R. Murrow are a few that come to mind.

The masses, by definition, are average. They are you and me. If you can figure out a way to sell to you and me, you can figure out an equally tasteful, clever, interesting way to sell to them.

# HOW TO USE THE TECHNIQUES THAT MAKE

# CLASSIC ADS CLASSIC TO MAKE GOOD ADS

# GREAT AND BAD ADS BETTER

## 16

The ads reprinted and critiqued in the following pages clearly and vividly illustrate the creative principles and techniques I've been discussing. Without them, any discussion of "innovative" or "provocative" advertising would remain largely theoretical. However, there is a danger in selecting certain ads as examples. Inexperienced readers may be inclined to scrutinize them in search of rules or formulas that can be applied to all advertising.

You should not view these ads as examples to imitate in a specific way. Approach them both as generalized demonstrations of a way of approaching creativity in advertising and as illustrations of a set of perceptions about the way words and pictures can be combined for maximum impact.

Most of the ads reprinted in black and white in the following pages were originally published in color. I have referred to the effective use of color in certain of the ads; if you find those references frustrating or confusing, I suggest you check out the original. A few minutes with the *Standard Directory of Advertisers* and the *Standard Directory of Advertising Agencies* (popularly known as the "Red Books") should give you the name, address, and telephone number of the appropriate agency, along with the names and titles of their top executives.

## NIKON

This ad, one in a series of ads created for an award-winning campaign for Nikon lenses, could be called a celebrity endorsement campaign—with a twist.

Eric Meola is a well-known advertising photographer. The two-page spread below surrounds one of Meola's most famous pictures with huge black quotation marks. Even without the third page of copy, this ad could stand on its own as a superb example of what can be done not only with Nikon lenses, but by a brilliant art director–writer team. The headline in the upper left, "Eric Meola on Nikon lenses:" used with the quotes surrounding the picture, is a dramatic, telegraphic way of showing rather than saying that Meola does his brilliant work with Nikon lenses. No other copy is necessary, since this famous picture, taken in 1977 and called "Promised Land," speaks for itself.

No explanation is needed for the metaphoric comment on American taste, or lack of it, made by the immense, white 1959 Cadillac fins, sticking out of a red and white garage that's too short, framed by a blue sky. The white Cadillac, the glaring red doors, and the white garage building, framed by two triangles of cobalt blue on top and black on the bottom, are sure to capture any reader's eye.

The copy identifying Meola, the picture (lower left, in mouse type), and Nikon is set out of the way, so as not to diminish the impact of the startling picture, but it says everything that has to be said.

The creative team combined the very essence of photographic art with type and copy to make the simplest, shortest, most dramatic statement possible about the quality of Nikon lenses and the pros who use them. "This," the big black quotes seem to say, "is all you have to know about how good Nikon lenses are, and the kind of job they do for famous photographers and can also do for you.

The third page provides details for people who want them. It picks up the motif of the huge black quote marks, which help draw attention to the copy in the same way they drew attention to the photograph. The two lenses Meola mentions using are shown discretely at the bottom of the ad. Notice, too, that Meola's words are also set much larger than the regular copy at the bottom of the ad. Meola, not the product, remains the star of the ad. Why? Because the more Meola's celebrity is emphasized, the more impressively it reflects upon the Nikon products he uses.

Note also that there are no cute, gimmicky art director tricks here—no fake laser beams, no hokey, heavily retouched close-up picture of lenses taken with star filters. They would cheapen the look of the ad and tarnish Nikon's quality image.

This ad is uncluttered, uncomplicated, and tasteful. The implicit message communicated to the reader is one of quality.

## APPLE COMPUTERS

Since computers are serious, expensive products, most computer advertising is serious. Much of it is also dull. Not Apple advertising. From the beginning, Apple ads have looked interesting and been fun to read because of their handsome, stylish layouts and playful use of language.

The long copy in this ad is broken up by interesting subheads. Most of them use the same type of play on words that is used in the headline. Notice that no people are shown in this ad; everything is focused on the product and the peripherals that come with it. Such an ad could seem sterile—and most computer ads are. But the way this ad is written, together with the warm brown desk and bookcase and the soft yellow-orange desk lamp in the main illustration, give it a friendly, inviting feeling.

Apple has always taken great care to give their advertising the same kind of "user-friendly" characteristics their computers possess. This ad is no exception. The implicit message here is that the IIc, like all Apple products (and unlike many forbidding, scientific-looking competitors) is *accessible*. Part of that message comes from the way the copy is written and part from the way the ad is laid out. It is neat, orderly, and handsome, but not so neat that it looks cold.

The main illustration is very important in this respect. It shows what seems to be an informal shot of a typical student's home study area. But the shot is anything but informal; it is composed with exquisite care. Notice the half-drunk glass of milk, the gerbil cage, the sunglasses carelessly inserted into the empty coffee cup alongside some pencils that could easily scratch the lenses. A small note taped to the bookshelf says, "math test Tuesday." This picture not only warms up the ad, it makes the ad interesting to look at because it contrasts so strongly with the formal silhouetted illustrations scattered throughout the copy. Subtly, nonverbally, the picture—and therefore the entire ad—reminds the reader how easily an Apple IIc would fit into a student's daily routine.

## SCALI, MCCABE, SLOVES, INC. (HOUSE AD): THE ART OF SHOWING OFF GRACEFULLY

House ads—the ads agencies run on their own behalf in order to attract clients—are essentially boasts. The problem is how to boast without sounding obnoxious or pretentious. The solution is to boast in such a disarming and charming way that you hardly seem to be boasting at all.

# TWO OUT OF THREE AIN'T BAD.

SAM SCALI
Inducted into the Art Director's
Hall of Fame, 1984

ED McCABE
Inducted into the Copy Hall of Fame,
1974

MARVIN SLOVES

All of us at Scali, McCabe, Sloves would like to congratulate Sam Scali on his induction into the Art Director's Hall of Fame.

We're very proud.

We're also proud of the fact that Sam is not alone. He joins his partner, Ed McCabe, who entered the Copy Hall of Fame in 1974.

And that makes Scali, McCabe, Sloves something very rare indeed: an advertising agency with two founding partners in the Hall of Fame.

Both of these men are advertising legends for good reason. Together, they have created some of the most renowned advertising of all time.

If you're interested in talking to a great art director or a great copywriter about your advertising, Sam and Ed aren't hard to find. They still come to work every day.

Or, if you'd like to talk to the person who does most of the talking for Sam and Ed, call Marvin.

There is, unfortunately, no such thing as a Management Hall of Fame.

But Marvin Sloves is a great reason for creating one.

## SCALI, McCABE, SLOVES, INC.

800 Third Avenue, New York, N.Y. 10022 (212) 421-2050 Offices in: Houston, Melbourne, Montreal, Toronto, London, Düsseldorf, Mexico City

This award-winning, full-page black-and-white ad for Scali, McCabe, Sloves ran in the *New York Times* on December 6, 1984. It has become something of a classic among house ads, which are notoriously difficult to write.

The headline refers to the fact that Sam Scali, like Ed McCabe, is now a member of the Advertising Hall of Fame. Instead of boasting about that by showing a big picture of Sam, or Sam and Ed, which might have seemed immodest, the headline takes an entirely different and quite intriguing tack—it almost seems to make fun of partner Marvin Sloves. Sam and Ed are provided with laurel wreaths, while Marvin is not. The use of a hoary device like laurel wreaths helps make the ad provocative, especially when it's combined with a headline using the word "ain't." In an old-fashioned way, laurel wreaths smack of dignity and seriousness. The use of common slang in combination with the wreaths not only catches the eye because they are conflicting symbols, it arouses the reader's curiosity still further by hinting that there may be more to this headline–visual combination than meets the eye. And why on earth, the reader might wonder, would an advertising agency, presumably dedicated to the art and craft of fine writing, be so brazen or careless as to use the word "ain't"?

I have mentioned *the quality of the unexpected* that characterizes most great ads. You'd expect an ad agency that has had a principal inducted into an honorary professional society to take an ad full of portentous blather about the beauty and power of the written word. In half pretending to celebrate Sam and Ed by playfully denigrating Marvin, SMS took an entirely different, refreshing, and completely *unexpected* approach—an approach that was bound to attract readers' attention.

Note also that although the ad appears at first glance to be making fun of Marvin Sloves, it winds up complimenting him and, by inference, the agency. Although no Management Hall of Fame exists, "Marvin Sloves," the last line reads, "is a great reason for creating one."

## MCCALL'S

*The Problem: McCall's* was thought of as a dull, drab, boring magazine, read by dull, drab, boring housewives. These award-winning posters showed huge, startling close-ups of Yoko Ono, Tina Turner, and Cher, among other female celebrities, who claimed they read the magazine. The headlines used *ironic counterpoint* to get across the idea that *McCall's* readers are not dull, drab housewives.

Another campaign, which went into more detail about the specific stories and service features each issue of the magazine contained, ran simultaneously with this campaign.

Several things make these ads especially provocative. First, the celebrities are not named. In some cases it takes the reader or viewer a moment or two to identify them, but most of them are such big stars, with such well-known faces, that they do not need to be identified. In either case, their faces attract immediate attention because the reader does not expect a famous face to be pictured alongside the words *dull* and *drab*. The combination attracts attention because it is unexpected. The large size of the close-ups of the celebrities also helps draw attention to the ads. And the simple, bold graphic, without a lot of copy, makes these ads inviting to read.

You might call this campaign an example of highly sophisticated celebrity endorsements, with a twist.

## CREST

This print campaign for Crest has won awards and helped sell Crest for years. None of these ads look like conventional toothpaste ads, which show beautiful, smiling children or close-ups of sexy young adults. Notice that all the visuals are simple and uncluttered—and unusual. In each case, the provocative headline–visual combination begins to tell a story that involves the benefits Crest offers. The reader gets some idea of what that story is about, but he is not given every detail. He has to do some work, reading the copy, which is short, to find out exactly what the ad is getting at. The copy is short because most consumers are familiar with Crest's benefits; the purpose of the ad is not so much to inform as to remind them.

The message in all these ads is simply that Crest helps prevent cavities. It is not always easy to dramatize a benefit involving prevention, not only because by its nature prevention represents the absence of something, but because the concept of *prevention* is an abstraction. That is why, in every case, the headline–visual combination uses concrete objects that seem to represent concrete ideas. A model of a tooth or a candy bowl may seem like a rather mundane object, but when it is made part of a short story that tells a reader how to save his teeth, it becomes very interesting.

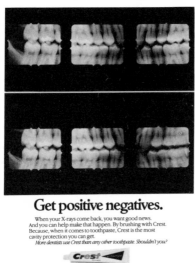

**Get positive negatives.**

When your X-rays come back, you want good news. And you can help make that happen. By brushing with Crest. Because, when it comes to toothpaste, Crest is the most cavity protection you can get.
*More dentists use Crest than any other toothpaste. Shouldn't you?*

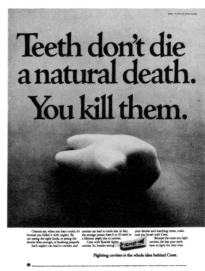

# Teeth don't die a natural death. You kill them.

Fighting cavities is the whole idea behind Crest.

## VOLKSWAGEN

What's true of a number of other ads is true of these classic VW ads: One of the most notable things about them was what they lacked—smiling young families, beautiful women draped over the hood, a neat little house with a manicured lawn and a white picket fence, and all the other clichés that characterized auto advertising in the 1960s and 1970s—and that continue to characterize certain auto ads even now.

Auto companies used to do everything they could to portray their cars as bigger than they really were, because consumers associated size with quality and status. That made "Think Small"—a reverse twist on the phrase "think big"—particularly appropriate. And showing the VW small, surrounded by a sea of white space, drew attention to the car. Since the car itself was small, it was appropriate to show it that way. Notice the way the copy is set—in three small, neat blocks. The neat, spare look of the layout, and the layouts of all the ads in the VW campaign, helped create an aura of engineering excellence about the VW; it was almost as though the ads themselves were well engineered.

**Think small.**

Ten years ago, the first Volkswagens were imported into the United States.

These strange little cars with their beetle shapes were almost unknown.

All they had to recommend them was 32 miles to the gallon (regular gas, regular driving), an aluminum air-cooled rear engine that would go 70 mph all day without strain, sensible size for a family and a sensible price tag too.

Beetles multiply; so do Volkswagens. By 1954,

VW was the best-selling imported car in America. It has held that rank each year since. In 1959, over 150,000 Volkswagens were sold, including 30,000 station wagons and trucks.

Volkswagen's snub nose is now familiar in fifty states of the Union, as American as apple strudel. In fact, your VW may well be made with Pittsburgh steel stamped out on Chicago presses (even the power for the Volkswagen plant is supplied by coal from the U.S.A.).

As any VW owner will tell you, Volkswagen service is excellent and it is everywhere. Parts are plentiful, prices low. (A new fender, for example, is only $21.75.*) No small factor in Volkswagen's success. Today, in the U.S.A. and 119 other countries, Volkswagens are sold faster than they can be made. Volkswagen has become the world's fifth largest automotive manufacturer by thinking small. More and more people are thinking the same.

*Suggested retail price.

These ads and other famous VW ads helped turn the Beetle into an irreverent, antiestablishment symbol for young people who had to watch their pennies and who were more interested in a simple, rugged, reliable, high-quality, no-frills car than in fins, power, and status.

The word *lemon* in relation to a car means, of course, that there are so many things wrong with it that it's practically worthless. The car in the "lemon" ad looked perfect. The reader was puzzled—why did the headline call a perfectly good car a lemon? The copy explained that a blemish on the chrome strip on the glove compartment had caught inspector Kurt Kroner's eye, so he sent the car back to be repaired. In other words, the standards of workmanship at VW were so high, VW considered a perfect car with the slightest blemish to be a virtual "lemon."

**Lemon.**

This Volkswagen missed the boat.

The chrome strip on the glove compartment is blemished and must be replaced. Chances are you wouldn't have noticed it; Inspector Kurt Kroner did.

There are 3,389 men at our Wolfsburg factory with only one job: to inspect Volkswagens at each stage of production. (3000 Volkswagens are produced daily; there are more inspectors

than cars.)

Every shock absorber is tested (spot checking won't do!), every windshield is scanned. VWs have been rejected for surface scratches barely visible to the eye.

Final inspection is really something! VW inspectors run each car off the line onto the Funktionsprüfstand (car test stand), tote up 189 check points, gun ahead to the automatic

brake stand, and say "no" to one VW out of fifty.

This preoccupation with detail means the VW lasts longer and requires less maintenance, by and large, than other cars. (It also means a used VW depreciates less than any other car.)

We pluck the lemons; you get the plums.

"Lemon" is a perfect example of an ad that is provocative because the creative team has left something out. The ad provides the reader with an illustration (A) and a headline (C), which, taken together, arouse the reader's curiosity. He is confronted with what psychologists call "cognitive dissonance"—the things he sees placed together don't make sense together. It puzzles him. To solve the puzzle—or, as I've put it elsewhere, to resolve the tension—he provides (B) by reading the copy. He becomes a participant, involved in finding out why the advertiser refers to a perfectly good car as a lemon.

Actually, in this context, *lemon* is an inappropriate word. The proper word for a car that does not pass factory inspection is *reject*. A headline that said "reject" would have worked for this ad, but not nearly as well as "lemon," because "reject" isn't nearly as damning and all-inclusive as "lemon." Calling the car a "lemon" is an example of the use of exaggeration for dramatic effect.

## MAXWELL HOUSE COFFEE

I spoke with Peter Barnet, Ogilvy & Mather Group director for General Foods, the maker of Maxwell House, about this commercial. Peter described its background and purpose, and the philosophy behind it:

This advertising breaks the mold of traditional coffee advertising in the U.S. The commercials consist of vignettes keyed to the music. The selling line, which is sung, is "Maxwell House fresh flavor . . . is coffee made our way." The historical signature, "Good to the last drop," is there as well. The vignettes show people of both sexes and all walks of life, over the age of twenty, enjoying themselves while they work, play, talk, or walk. They are big, short, tall, fat, and thin. They are doing ordinary things, but in a way that has some joy and surprise in it. Certain close-ups, of a smiling, middle aged man and a very attractive older blond woman with a lined face, are repeated, so audiences will get to know them and will identify each of several commercials in the series with the others.

Historically, there has been very little movement of individual coffee brands that you can attribute to advertising. The coffee business is driven by commodity pricing in the grocery stores. People switch on price on a regular basis. Basically, within the two or three

top brands, most consumers feel they're about the same. The question is, what role do you want advertising to play? Can you become more ambitious with it? Can you turn advertising into an offensive weapon for growth? We've tried to do that with these commercials.

Let's face it, coffee is an "old shoe" product; in our view, people are largely bored with coffee advertising. How do you breathe life and new energy into it? You try to tell them, in an entertaining, contemporary way, that your brand is their kind of coffee for their kind of people. It's the choice of a lot of people with whom they identify, who they would like to emulate, and who seem to enjoy life in a way with which they empathize.

The high ground in advertising today, we believe, is relevancy rather than product-based points of difference, which, increasingly, may be meaningless to people. What makes a brand different, in our view, does not necessarily make it more attractive. In advanced countries like ours, the line between food and entertainment is thin or nonexistent. Think about what you want from a restaurant. Dining out is more than food, it's an experience, an entertaining thing to do. I don't think that traditional coffee advertising has done a good enough job of making people feel that going through life every day without a good cup of coffee is really missing out on something.

This advertising tries to say, "Maxwell House is America's coffee, it's the best coffee," in a manner that demonstrates how well that coffee fits in with your everyday enjoyment of life. That's why we see ordinary people, but they have a certain spark, a certain enjoyment of what they're doing, and Maxwell House, we are trying to say, is part of that. This is advertising designed to make people feel happy about what they're watching, happy about coffee, and happy about Maxwell House. It's a bit of "love my advertising, love my brand."

This was recall tested and it got a fairly good recall score. But all coffee recall scores are low and Maxwell House has historically been low. This recalled better than most. It went national before it was recall tested. We believe it has created greater involvement, in greater depth, with Maxwell House coffee advertising than we have seen in the past.

## OBSESSION

What does a campaign for a perfume have to do? Get attention for the perfume in a relevant way. It should be provocative enough, interesting and fresh enough, to cause talk. Most perfume advertising tries to do that by using conventional photographs to dramatize typically romantic or mildly sexy situations and implying or stating directly that a given brand of perfume will heighten the romance by making the woman more alluring.

The trouble is that perfume companies, apparently a rather conventional lot, tend to stick with mundane approaches. Since there is nothing particularly bold or daring about the words and pictures they use and the way the words and pictures relate to each other, most perfume ads don't cause much talk or attract much attention.

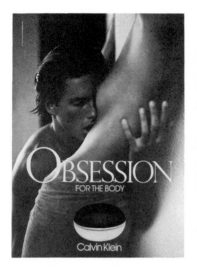  

These Obsession ads go much farther than most perfume ads. They "stretch the envelope," as test pilots say, mostly because they appear to be extremely explicit. If you examine them closely, however, you will see that only one shows part of a woman's breast and nipple. The others are suggestive, but it is impossible to see exactly what parts of the models' bodies are visible, or what the models are supposed to be doing. There is nothing explicitly "dirty" or graphic in any of these ads; the mechanisms they use to attract attention are not "dirty pictures," but nuance and subtle suggestion. In the most explicit ad, a model is resting his face against a woman's breast and stomach. In the other, the male model appears to be kissing the woman's finger. In the third ad, a small group of women appear to be lying together on a towel. Certainly, in these days of *Hustler* and *Penthouse* and porno video rental tapes, the situations *as they are literally depicted* are quite tame.

Two of the ads have an overall blue-gray tone that makes them different from any other perfume ads I've seen. And two have a scratched, marred surface, which gives them a mysterious cast that also makes them different from any ads I have ever seen for any product. In each case the photograph runs off the edge of the page, making the photo seem bigger than it really is.

These ads excite the reader's imagination in a much more timely and contemporary way than ordinary perfume ads do. The campaign helps set Obsession apart from other perfumes because the ads look different from ordinary perfume ads. They're wilder, more passionate, more intense, more suggestive—in short, more contemporary.

## PIE À LA ANY MODE

Three things make this trade ad so successful, and so unusual: (1) the sense of playfulness in the headline–visual combination; (2) the huge size of the headline in contrast with the tiny pie charts; and (3) the neat, attractive way the ad is laid out.

The pie charts were printed in various shades of green, yellow, orange, purple, and blue, against a black background. By placing the charts, and the headline (printed in thick, white type) against black, the art director made them "pop." The thick, bold type style makes the headline and subhead easy to read, even though they are printed in reverse.

This ad contains a great deal of information, some of it highly technical. It also contains a free offer. The subhead, which contains a great deal of important information, could have served as the headline. But that would have made this ad look like every other trade ad.

By using the double entendre "pie à la any mode" along with the pie charts, the creative team created a headline–visual combination that is unusually provocative, especially for a trade ad. True, the ad is a bit slower than it would be if the headline were "straighter" or more direct, but it is also more fun to read.

Notice, by the way, that although the product and product name are not shown in large type, they are prominently displayed. And a great deal of information is tucked down at the bottom, below the double ruled lines, to keep the ad from looking cluttered.

## MY FIRST SONY

This provocative, innovative, and very tasteful ad is deceptive. It is powerful because it is so simple, even rather plain-looking. It does a number of things successfully: It positions the product line; it shows four different products, each of them twice; it gives the reader a sense of the size of each of the products; and it shows how the products are used.

Note that although the ad announces a new product line, the words *new* and *announcing* are not used. They would make this ad seem stale—the last thing Sony wanted in an ad announcing a fresh new line of products was the kind of ad that reads "Announcing A New Line Of High Quality Audio Products For Kids" or something equally obvious.

There are no double meanings and no word play as such, but the rhythm of the headline makes it lively and charming, and therefore interesting to read.

Instead of being shown in typical, hackneyed play situations, the children are posed in a fairly conventional way against a blank background. The background helps focus the reader's attention on the children's faces and the bright red products they're holding.

When appropriate, print and TV advertising should have a sense of playfulness. That does not mean the people shown in the illustrations or photographs must literally be playing. The playfulness and fun can come from the wording of the headline, the look on the models' faces, or the way they are posed; from the illustration; or from the way the headline and the visual fit together. This sense of playfulness helps the ads stand out from other, more serious and straightforward ads. In a cerebral way, it also helps the ad come alive. What happens is hard to describe precisely; it is as though the ad lifts itself an inch or two off the page and hangs in the air, inviting—indeed, almost demanding—that the reader pay attention to it.

After years of giving people smaller electronics, Sony now makes electronics for smaller people.

Starting now, people who aren't fully grown up can have electronics that are. Because Sony is introducing My First Sony™—audio products that are tough on the outside, but Sony on the inside. (Why should tiny ears have to listen to tiny sound?) So the Walkman® personal stereo is every note a Sony. And the rest of the line also brings you Sony quality in kid's sizes: the Sing Along Cassette Player with Microphone, the **SONY.**

easy-to-tote Radio Cassette-Corder, and the hands-free Walkie-Talkie. What's more, our durable designs have been created especially for your creations. The controls are child-sized, and other thoughtful features include protective rubber accents and a volume limiter on the Walkman personal stereo. Indeed, it's only fitting that after years of creating electronics that represent the next generation, Sony now turns its attention to the younger generation.

**my first Sony**®

There is an artfully conceived, subtle sense of play in this ad. It comes from the playful way the headline is written and the way the kids are posed. The basic sense of this ad is playful, but the playfulness is restrained because the ad's explicit purpose is quite serious. Because the execution is so artful, the ad works a lot harder and is a lot more clever than it seems at first glance.

## BARTLES & JAYMES WINE COOLER

The commercials in this campaign feature the mythical Frank Bartles and his partner Ed Jaymes, who never speaks. In this spot, Frank, acting the *naif*, talks to us from a Jewish deli. He refers to bagels as "big doughnuts" and lox as "fish." In his usual charming, down-home manner, he explains that his wine cooler goes just as well with big doughnuts and fish as it does with many other kinds of food. We are invited to laugh—gently—at Frank and Ed because they apparently don't know the difference between lox and bagels and fish and doughnuts. The actors play the part of small-town hicks in the big city, earnestly trying to convince the viewer of the attributes of their wine cooler, while "thanking" the viewer "for your support" the way a local politician might thank the voters assembled in the local high school gym for listening to him speak.

"Continuing characters" like these—fictitious characters, created by an agency, who appear in all the advertising for a particular brand, like Mr. Whipple for Charmin and Mrs. Olsen for Folger's coffee—provide consumers with a "hook," something that reminds them of the product and makes them feel familiar with it, so they will be more likely to reach for it on a supermarket shelf full of similar, competitively priced items.

### BARTLES & JAYMES WINE COOLER
"Bagels"
:30 Commercial

FRANK: Hello. This is Frank Bartles speaking to you from New York City.

As many of you know, the Bartles & Jaymes Premium Wine Cooler is not only perfect as a refreshment, . . . but with meals as well.

Ed says it even goes with these big doughnuts they like to eat here.

I personally would not have thought Bartles & Jaymes and doughnuts would go together, much less doughnuts and fish.

But I have tried it myself, and once again, Ed is right.

So please continue to enjoy Bartles & Jaymes with all kinds of food, and we thank you once more for your support.

Traditionally, continuing characters have been used, usually in packaged goods commercials, to personalize a point of difference or symbolize a sense of enhanced quality or value. In certain cases, these fake characters and the actors who play them become mini-celebrities. When that happens, any commercial containing the character becomes hard to beat in twenty-four-hour recall tests, because viewers' recall in each new spot tends to be reinforced by the characters' appearances in all the other spots that have been broadcast over the years.

Many creative people feel these made-up characters insult viewers' intelligence because they are usually corny, trite, and stereotyped. But Frank and Ed (like the famous Maytag repairman) prove that continuing characters do not have to be insipid and dull, nor do they have to offend the sensibilities of the more sophisticated members of the viewing audience in order to sell products. They can, in fact, be as charming and innovative as they are memorable.

The Bartles & Jaymes spots are memorable because they are fresh and witty, artfully conceived and beautifully written, acted, and produced. Unlike traditional continuing character campaigns, these spots do not force the viewer to listen to one stilted copy point after another coming from the mouth of a tough-talking waitress, a female plumber, a foxy grandpa, or sweet little grandma. Since viewers are made to feel they are in on the joke, so to speak, they do not feel they are being treated like imbeciles, and they tend to react with pleasure toward the product being advertised. In other words, the Bartles & Jaymes commercials make sales by making friends. You might say that Frank and Ed are to ordinary continuing characters what "Hill Street Blues" and "Moonlighting" are to ordinary cop and detective shows.

Notice that there are no dubious claims in these commercials—nothing is "brewed with live steam" or "all natural," nothing contains "X-27" or "flavor puffs." The wine cooler audience is assumed to be too sophisticated for such stuff. Notice too, that Ed never talks. Why? Nobody knows. He just doesn't. Who ever heard of a continuing character in a TV commercial who is on camera for the entire length of the commercial and never says a word? Nobody. That's one of the things that makes these commercials unique and memorable—and, ultimately, so powerful.

The question, then, is not whether continuing characters are more or less effective than some other executional device. The question is: How can you use such a device—or any device, for that matter—in a fresh, memorable way? How can you use it to make sales by making friends for your product? There is no simple answer, of course. But all the possible answers begin with a client who adopts a flexible, receptive point of view to fresh, innovative types of executions and witty, imaginative variations of traditional, stereotyped executional devices.

## COFFEE GROWERS OF COLOMBIA

The Venice-Simplon Orient Express, the word's most luxurious train, serves 100 percent Colombian coffee exclusively. On this trip, they run out of coffee, and since they wouldn't think of serving anything less than "the richest coffee in the world," the train heads back to Paris.

This brief, disarming, tongue-in-cheek spot dramatizes the point—Colombian coffee's high quality—by exaggerating its importance to the passengers and the people who run the train.

It must be a Colombian Coffee break.

The richest coffee in the world."

"Exaggerating the negative"—dramatizing a situation in which consumers fail to benefit from the product, or suffer because they haven't obtained it, instead of showing them enjoying its benefits—is an excellent way to create effective advertising with a memorable message. Even so, many advertisers refuse to try it because they fear, usually without justification, that viewers will associate their product with the negative aspects of the dramatization.

"Good taste," which is what Colombian coffee offers, is extremely difficult to dramatize—it's an abstraction. Most advertisers take the safe, happy, dull way out: They resort to portraying happy families at dinner who compliment Mom on her cooking, or handsome couples smiling at each other over the breakfast table or on a date in a fancy restaurant. This commercial is much more fun to watch. It avoids all the clichés and, in the bargain, adds a bit of glamor and allure to the product by using a well-known, classy foreign location. What's more, in its own charming way, it presents viewers with an impressive testimonial for Colombian coffee by making it clear, amid all the fun, that Colombian is the coffee that is actually used on the Orient Express.

We know why they're here.

The tone of the two print ads is equally offbeat and interesting. They are far more oblique and subtle, and therefore far more interesting, than most print ads for coffee. One ad shows an empty commodities exchange and implies, in its ironic way, that the reason it is empty is that the traders have discovered that Colombian coffee is being served during the coffee break. Every last one of them has rushed off to have a cup. The second ad features a large photograph of a flying saucer. The whimsical headline implies that visitors from outer space have been visiting Earth in order to pick up some Colombian coffee.

In advertising, less is almost always more. The more quickly and cleverly you can dramatize your point, the more powerful your advertising is likely to be. These ads do more than avoid the usual clichés. By using striking visuals and terse, ironic headlines, they appeal to their affluent, sophisticated, well-educated target audience. The agency has used clever, interesting advertising to impart a clever, interesting personality to the coffee—the type of personality upscale buyers are likely to respond to. This is done by implication; the phrase "sophisticated taste" or "high quality" never appear in the ads. The phrase "The richest coffee in the world" does appear in tiny type at the bottom of the ads, but that is the only direct reference to quality in the ads. (Many clients insist their logos be printed relatively large, so readers will be sure to notice them. The problem is, since logos are basically signs, they are usually neither charming nor interesting, and at best are only slightly informative. In addition, the larger they are, the more likely they are to distract the reader from a provocative head-line–visual combination, and to get in the way of the story the ad is trying to dramatize.)

Like the VW ads, these headline–visuals leave something out. The reader's attention is attracted by a picture of a flying saucer (A). He looks for a headline to explain this strange picture. The headline (C) says cryptically, "We know why they're here." The reader is slightly puzzled. He asks himself who it is who is supposed to know why flying saucer people are visiting Earth. Then his eye falls on the logo and the tagline, and they give him the hint (B) he needs to solve the puzzle. "OH!" he says to himself, in effect, "I get it. It's the *Colombian coffee people* who know why the spacemen are here—to pick up some Colombian coffee and take it back to their own planet!" (My description sounds simplistic. But the process I am describing, which occurs in a fraction of a second, is what makes a great deal of the most provocative advertising so involving, so stimulating, so memorable, and ultimately so powerful.)

When the reader gets the joke, he gets the ad's message. But unlike what happens with more explicit ads—which, as I have pointed out, tend not to involve the reader because they read more like speeches than like plays—he has, in effect, given himself the message. Since he has become involved in doping it out, he is more likely to remember the ad and to respond favorably to similar ads in the future.

## ABSOLUT, CHIVAS REGAL, AND CROWN ROYAL

How do you break through the clutter of whiskey ads? By making your whiskey

**ABSOLUT SCHARF.**

**ABSOLUT WARHOL.**

ad seem different from conventional "Yuppie in the penthouse" ads. And by making your ads say what they have to say—that your whiskey is the kind of high-quality, classy, with-it whiskey that affluent, successful, attractive, knowledgeable people drink—in a provocative way.

The best way to do that, if you can manage it, is by implication. It is uncool to try to convince other people you're cool by telling them how cool you are. The ads that work best convey a sense of quality and class in the way they go about making their claim, instead of by making an explicit claim. When the reader comes across these lighthearted, good-natured ads he says to himself, without thinking consciously about it: "This manufacturer expresses himself, or calls attention to himself, in the same clever way I would if I were advertising this product. He's my kind of guy. His whiskey is my kind of whiskey. If I see his brand in a friend's home, I'll know my friend knows his whiskey and appreciates the finer things. The next time I need Scotch or vodka, I'll try this brand."

**What else would you give a special Daddy for Father's Day?**

Daddy Warbucks © 1985 Tribune Media Services, Inc.
Chivas Regal © 1985 375 Spirits Co., N.Y.C. 12 Years Old Worldwide · Blended Scotch Whisky · 86 Proof

In other words, the way the ads say what they have to say reassures the reader that this is indeed classy hooch, in the same way fancy clothes or a fancy car sends signals that the wearer or driver is a knowledgeable, successful, tasteful person. Although they go about it in a much more whimsical fashion, these ads create a personality for each brand in exactly the same way the Marlboro campaign has created a macho personality for the cigarette.

In the case of "Absolut Scharf" and "Absolut Warhol" one could argue that many readers would not understand the reference to the artists Andy Warhol and Kenny Scharf. It is not crucial if one ad in a campaign of fifteen or twenty is a bit obscure, as long as it is attractive enough to catch the eye and is recognizable as part of a familiar campaign. The cumulative effect of the entire campaign is what is most important. Besides, ads that reproduce actual paintings by well-known artists add a touch of prestige, snob appeal, and glamor to the brand.

The "Daddy Warbucks" Father's Day ad for Chivas Regal is one in a long series of outstanding ads that have helped build the brand. Most Chivas Regal ads show a large picture of the bottle with a clever, often whimsical headline. This ad, one of the most unusual and charming holiday whiskey ads I have seen, is especially memorable because it is so visually innovative. It has a delightfully unexpected "fish-in-the-face" quality. Daddy Warbucks is an especially appropriate cartoon character, of course, because he is supposed to be a multibillionaire who is used to the finer things in life.

The "Jill is dating some guy from L.A." ad for Crown Royal is as innovative visually, in its way, as the Chivas Regal and Absolut ads. (It may not be apparent in reproduction, but the copy is stitched into fabric in the same way those old-

fashioned "Home Sweet Home" wall samplers used to be.) This ad may even be considered a bit more daring than the others because it fails to show either the bottle or the label. By implication, the hip, sophisticated copy helps create a contemporary personality for the brand. It could be argued that the ad is weak because it does not convey any explicit, meaningful information to the consumer about the brand. Even the Chivas Regal ad, far out as it is, implies that Chivas is an expensive, high-quality Scotch suitable for people who are rich enough not to have to compromise.

I think this argument has some validity. But on a more sophisticated plane, it seems to me that premium whiskey drinkers, like cigarette smokers and sports car buyers, tend to favor brands that have a bold, adventurous image. I would argue that, by implication, the mere fact that this ad is as innovative as it is, both visually and verbally, adds a feeling of boldness and adventurousness to the brand's image.

## BMW

Many of the ads in this chapter contain headline–visual combinations that use double meanings or word plays to be provocative. Many are whimsical.

Provocative ads are not always whimsical, and they do not always involve double entendres or word plays. In many cases bold, straightforward statements of fact make extremely provocative headlines, especially when the type face and graphic treatment add to the drama the words possess.

This ad introduced readers to the fact that certain BMW models were equipped with ABS braking. (ABS uses a computer to help avoid skidding and to stop your car more quickly when you slam on the brakes, especially on wet pavement.) As the ad points out, ABS is the same system huge jet liners use to help bring them to a stop safely and quickly when they land. The phrase "two of the world's foremost authorities" used at the beginning of the headline on the first page help give the ad an aura of importance. And the phrase "on acceleration" followed by "in deceleration" gives the line a rhythm that makes it interesting to read.

The dramatic picture of the car, dwarfed by the jet engine in the spread, uses the stark contrast between the two objects to attract the reader's attention. A car usually dominates the page in an ad, because readers think of cars as fairly large objects and expect to see them shown large. In this case, the art director put the car next to an object so large that the car actually looks small by comparison. Changing the context in which the viewer usually sees the car makes the car much more noticeable than it usually would be. It is not as apparent in this black-and-white reproduction, but in this photograph, which is washed in that characteristic, blue-gray light that seems to fill large open spaces like airports at dawn, the car's parking lights are on. This tiny bit of contrasting color helps draw the reader's eye toward the car.

In contrast to the two huge, contrasting structural masses on the left of the page, the copy, in a column on the right, is set quite small. The contrast adds drama to the page. The type style and size, and the layout of the ad, including its blue-gray tone, help set the ad apart from most other car ads—indeed, from most other ads of any kind. How many car ads have you seen that seem to eschew color almost entirely? Most car ads are splashed with vivid colors, because color, after all, is "beautiful." The problem is that all that color tends to make every car ad look like every other car ad. In this case, the art director used various shades of the same subdued color to catch the viewer's attention in an innovative way.

Although BMW bills itself as a luxury car loaded with advanced technology, it was not the first automobile to offer ABS braking. BMW needed a single, very powerful ad that would make their old news seem like big news. That's exactly what this ad did, both by comparing BMW's ABS to the ABS that stops giant airliners, and by the way they chose to compare them. The sophisticated techniques used by the creative team gave this award-winning ad the impact of an event.

## DUNKIN' DONUTS

This delightful, tongue-in-cheek thirty-second spot for Dunkin' Donuts' croissants is an excellent example of a commercial that gets its point across by *exaggerating the negative.*

The Dunkin' Donut man passes a group of "great pastry chefs," one of whom tastes the man's croissants and shouts in despair, "My life is over!" That is, Dunkin' Donuts' croissants taste so good that the chef's whole reason for being has been destroyed.

The point about the extraordinary quality of these croissants is made by exaggeration. There are no smiling Moms, no sappy-looking families ecstatically crying, "Mmmmmm!" The playlet dramatizes the point of high quality through the humorous use of conflict and contrast. Notice how much the Dunkin' Donut man looks like a weak, timid, put-upon soul, and how big and robust and well-fed the chefs look. The contrast in costuming and casting helps make the confrontation more dramatic—and therefore more humorous. Remember what Charlie Chaplin said about generating sympathy for the little tramp who is threatened by the big cop? The same thing happens here.

In the middle of the spot, we have the mandatory extreme product close-up, and the super, "Dunkin' Donuts' Croissants," to help the viewers remember the product, its name, and the sponsor's name. This spot may look simple to pull off—after all, there are only two main characters and some croissants on a set— but it is not. Speed and economy are central to effective humor in advertising. That means that to bring it off successfully, the writing, wardrobe, directing choreography, camera work, casting, and lighting must dovetail perfectly. This spot is actually quite complicated to shoot because it is crucial to integrate camera angles into the action that show the viewer the tasty-looking croissants without being obvious about it.

Dramatizing an exaggeration of the negative is a very effective device, used by many highly creative agencies to get the point across in TV commercials. It must be done with a deft hand and a light touch, however, so the humorous device does not distract the viewer or overwhelm the benefit the spot is designed to promote.

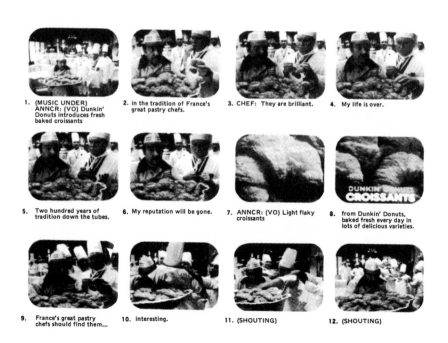

1. (MUSIC UNDER) ANNCR: (VO) Dunkin' Donuts introduces fresh baked croissants

2. in the tradition of France's great pastry chefs.

3. CHEF: They are brilliant.

4. My life is over.

5. Two hundred years of tradition down the tubes.

6. My reputation will be gone.

7. ANNCR: (VO) Light flaky croissants

8. from Dunkin' Donuts, baked fresh every day in lots of delicious varieties.

9. France's great pastry chefs should find them...

10. interesting.

11. (SHOUTING)

12. (SHOUTING)

Advertisers must be sophisticated enough to let a commercial flow in the organic way its creators intended—without demanding that their product be on screen for twenty seconds out of every thirty, or that supers spelling out product benefits be plastered over every scene. Notice that the product is on screen throughout the entire commercial, but it does not get in the way of the playlet's point—that these Dunkin' Donuts croissants taste so good, the envious French chef wants to kill the man who made them.

## JOHNNIE WALKER SCOTCH

This award-winning campaign for Johnnie Walker Black Label Scotch positions Johnnie Walker as a quality Scotch by comparing it to well-known artifacts created in the past by master artisans working for rich patrons. The copy justifies the high price of the Scotch. It says, in effect "If you want the best, you've got to pay for it—but it's worth it." You might call this campaign "successful borrowed interest," but it is actually much more than that.

Several things make these ads unique. First, they do not show the bottle or the box it comes in. For most clients, that is anathema. But product identification is not lacking; it has simply been accomplished in an unusual, provocative (and very tasteful) way. Setting the gold label against black at the center of the bottom of the ad, instead of showing it in a close-up on the side of the bottle, not only helps give the ads a distinctive visual identity, it helps instantly to set this campaign apart from most other whiskey advertising.

The use of color pictures of well-known, famous, beautiful objects gives the ads visual appeal. Not only does the short block of copy just above the label draw the eye toward the label, but its brevity makes it inviting to read.

Most important, the tone and phraseology of the copy in the headlines is light, casual, and conversational. It is not stiff, formal, or pretentious, as many whiskey headlines are. The contrast between the extremely formal, dramatically lit photographs and the casual, colloquial style of the copy in the headlines—the idea, for example, that Czar Nicholas would "quibble" with Carl Fabergé or Shah Jehan would even think of telling his "contractor" to "make the Taj Mahal pool a little smaller"—makes the headline–visual combination provocative.

By implication, the superb photography conveys a sense of quality. The subjects of the photographs also convey a sense of quality. But the concept behind the ads—comparing something as mundane as a bottle of whiskey, even a high-quality whiskey, to something as magnificent as the Taj Mahal, in a tongue-in-cheek way—is what makes these ads so unusual and effective.

# WENDY'S

This spot for Wendy's was shot by director Joe Sedelmaier. The point of the commercial is that hamburgers at Wendy's taste better because, unlike their competitors, they don't start to cook your burger until the moment you order it.

The point is made by dramatizing the negative. A hapless, hungry customer visits a competing burger parlor and, in a hilarious exchange, tries to find out why he can't get his burger freshly made at the time he orders it. The clerks explain that they make all their burgers an hour ahead of time, so the burger he wants at noon was made at eleven. Confused, the customer asks whether he has to appear at nine o'clock, breakfast time, in order to get fresh food at lunch.

The spot is shot with a locked-off camera and the various Sedelmaier touches—offbeat casting and little bits of business like the customer behind our hero who reaches around his neck to show him the time. The sponsor's name and product are shown at the end, allowing the customer's exasperation to build to the payoff line, "Look at it this way, you beat the noontime crowds."

The benefit Wendy's offers has been dramatized in an extremely provocative way—by showing us a little playlet in which the customer who shops for lunch someplace else is frustrated by personnel who are completely indifferent to his desires. The managers at the competing restaurants are more interested in their own "efficiency" than in serving their customers' needs. What is most unusual about this spot, aside from Sedelmaier's unique way of shooting, casting, and cutting it, is the fact that (a) it's funny in a whimsical, lighthearted way that's appropriate for a fast food chain; (2) it's simple and uncomplicated—there's no mistaking the point the commercial is trying to make; (3) it avoids all the clichés of fast food advertising such as long, loving close-ups of food being cooked and consumed, and quick cuts of handsome teenagers and attractive young families

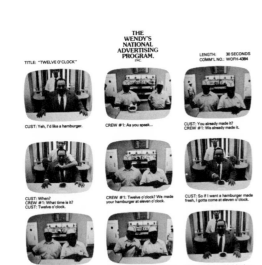

ecstatically munching burgers and swilling soda; and (4) unlike practically every other fast food commercial for the past ten years, nobody is singing and dancing on camera.

Notice that, although the humorous situation is wildly exaggerated, it is not forced, in that it is not a far-fetched attempt to be funny simply for the sake of being funny. All the fun is specifically focused on the problem you avoid when you visit Wendy's.

Unfortunately, many advertisers shy away from portraying negative situations for fear they will lose the audience's sympathy or offend some small segment. There's no chance of that happening here, because the humor is handled with great charm. Even the "bad guy" competitors are fun to watch and listen to.

## BARRON'S

Since business is a serious subject, many clients who advertise business magazines err on the side of being portentous and dull. Their claims, usually involving highly suspect interpretations of statistics that readers find fishy in the first place, tend to get lost in a welter of pictures of grand-looking silver-haired daddies wearing blue, pin-striped, three-piece suits; close-ups of top grain leather attaché cases; and long shots of black limousines on Park Avenue or Wall Street.

These *Barron's* ads provide a refreshing change. For one thing, they're not stuffy. In fact, they're fun to read. One of them uses a cartoon illustration by the famous *New Yorker* cartoonist Ed Koren. The illustration makes the ads more inviting to read by making them seem less like treatises or tomes and more like the brief, readable messages or short memos they resemble.

"Lowest cost per millionaire"—a twist on the media jargon, "lowest cost per million"—makes its point in an offbeat, whimsical, but quite relevant way. "Prosperity could be just around the corner," a repeat of the famous phrase from Depression days, takes on a double meaning when it's combined with Koren's drawing of a newsstand that seems to feature only *Barron's*. In its witty, upbeat, tongue-in-cheek way, the ad seems to be saying that the prosperity that people used to insist was "just around the corner" could literally be that, if you were

# Lowest cost per millionaire.

Ads like this usually congratulate themselves on their alluring cost-per-thousand figures.

And ours are more alluring than most: Barron's has a lower overall CPM than Business Week, Forbes or Fortune. Period.

But we point you now to a more revealing set of numbers—the sort that show up not on media plans but on personal statements of net worth.

Almost one third (31%) of Barron's readers come from households with a net worth of $1 million or more.* Which is substantially more than the competition.

That works out to a little more than two and a half cents a millionaire. Which is substantially *less* than the competition.

So if you're looking to reach an upscale audience, no one will take you to the top of that scale as effectively as Barron's.

And no one charges as little for the trip.

**BARRON'S**
HOW THE SMART MONEY
GETS THAT WAY.

---

to travel around the corner to your local newsstand and pick up a copy of *Barron's*.

The "captains" ad gives new life to the cliché "captains of industry" by adding "without paying for all the lieutenants." Having a bit of fun with a familiar phrase makes this headline provocative.

Notice that there is not much copy in these ads. The implicit message of the amusing headlines, the simple visuals, and the short blocks of copy is that *Barron's* is an accessible, easy-to-read newspaper that will help your business career. Without consciously thinking of it, the consumer makes a mental note to himself that since the ads are interesting and witty and attractive, it is likely that the newspaper they're advertising is, too. Notice also that in the two ads that do not show the newspaper—usually mandatory in advertising for publications sold mostly on newsstands and only secondarily by subscription—the newspaper is shown small, just above the artfully phrased tagline, "How The Smart Money Gets That Way."

Many publishers insist the entire front page of their newspaper or magazine be shown in their advertising. It seems logical to them to show what amounts to the package for their product,

# Buy the captains of industry without paying for all the lieutenants.

If you're very selective about target audiences, you've probably found that most magazines don't share your selectivity.

Yes, they'll deliver the upper-echelon types you need to reach—along with large numbers of those you don't. And every thousand you don't want will cost exactly as much as those you do.

The less comfortable you are with such inefficiencies, the more receptive you'll be to Barron's.

Because we deliver a higher concentration of people in top management earning six-figure incomes than Business Week, Forbes or Fortune.

And you needn't pay a premium to zero in on all that power and wealth.

In fact, we deliver that audience at a lower cost per thousand than any of our competitors.

That's why, in a time of declining industry ad sales, advertisers have bought more space in Barron's for two years running.

Rank has its privileges. In Barron's, you pay less for them.

**BARRON'S**
HOW THE SMART MONEY GETS THAT WAY

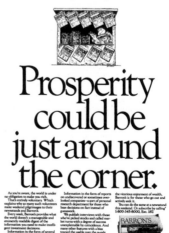

# Prosperity could be just around the corner.

As you're aware, the world is under no obligation to make you rich.

That's entirely voluntary. Which explains why so many such volunteers make weekend pilgrimages to their newsstands and Barron's.

Every week, Barron's provides what the world doesn't: a manageable and eminently readable digest of the information you need to make intelligent investment decisions.

Information in the form of several dozen pages of vital market statistics—a sort of personal data bank with virtually no limit on withdrawals.

Information in the form of reports on undiscovered or sometimes overlooked companies—a sort of personal research department for those who base decisions on fact instead of guesswork.

We publish interviews with those who've picked stocks and called markets' turns with a degree of success unexplainable by coincidence. And many other features with a bias toward the usable over the purely theoretical.

That's what sets Barron's apart. In a world of publications devoted to the vicarious enjoyment of wealth, Barron's is for those who go out and actively seek it.

You can do the same at a newsstand this weekend. Or subscribe by calling* 1-800-345-8000, Ext. 182.

HOW THE SMART MONEY
GETS THAT WAY

so that potential readers will be able to recognize the cover on the newsstand. The problem is that most magazine covers are not particularly useful for advertising purposes because they are designed to stand on their own, not to be integrated smoothly into an advertising layout.

The most important element on the cover is the title of the magazine. In each of the ads shown here, the issue of *Barron's* is shown folded. That way, it registers the name and the look of the cover without wasting a lot of space. The space that has been saved has been better used for large, provocative headlines, with a lot of leading between lines, to make them easy to read.

One of the reasons these ads are so good is that the word play and double meanings used in the headlines are easily understood; they have snap and vigor and are not forced or labored.

Other excellent business magazine campaigns are those currently running for *Forbes* (which I understand Malcolm Forbes has a hand in writing) and *The Wall Street Journal* (tagline: "The Daily Diary Of The American Dream").

## ESCORT RADAR DETECTORS

The phenomenal success of this very expensive, high-quality radar detector is due in no small part to years of highly effective direct-response advertising. The product is sold only by mail. All the ads in the long-running Escort campaign are like these two examples—full of long copy, with neat, clean layouts. The headlines are usually cleverly worded, but not too clever, and always very much to the point. Notice that each of the headlines refers to a specific fact. There is nothing vague in these ads. They are not precious or cute; the manufacturer knows that drivers take the subject of radar detectors very seriously. The tone of the headlines and copy and the neat, clean layouts inspire confidence and, by implication, promote the feeling that this is a precision product.

Unlike many competitive ads, there are no corny visual pyrotechnics here—no digitalized diagrams, no swoopy, stylized renditions of radar beams, no simulated laser light or other hackneyed high-tech symbols that would tend to trivialize the product and its claims.

There are also no pretty, smiling models staring happily at the reader from the seat of a Mercedes Benz 450 SL, and no goofy-looking drivers going ga-ga over the product. There is no cropped close-up of part of a Porsche 828 dashboard—a standard cliché of automotive aftermarket advertising.

The type size is not large, but there's a lot of leading, or "air," between sentences, which makes the copy seem easy to read.

The reader has the sense that the company that runs this ad has nothing to hide and can be trusted.

## MCDONALD'S BILLBOARD

This, in case you don't recognize it, is a McDonald's billboard. It uses the famous golden arch symbol to form the letter "m," then arranges the "m"s to form the expression "mmmmmmm," the way kids do when they're contemplating eating something they enjoy. The expression is printed on McDonald's familiar red background.

In a wonderfully whimsical, terse, clever way, this billboard informs passersby that there's a McDonald's nearby, offering delicious food. It presents its message the way kids might present it if they were writing and designing billboards—in a very bright, sprightly, refreshing way.

This is an absolutely masterful piece of advertising. It raises economy, compression, and impact to new heights. It's hard to imagine how any ad agency could create a more imaginative or effective billboard.

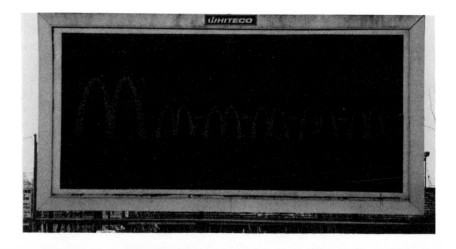

## NEW YORK AIR

The perennial problem in creating provocative airline advertising is avoiding clichés—handsome pilots cradling passengers' babies, smiling stewardesses fluffing pillows behind the heads of sweet old ladies or tired businesspeople, jumbo jets flying off into sunsets. The problem was even worse for New York Air, because its competitor, Eastern Airlines' shuttle, was famous, and the New York Airshuttle wasn't.

The team who created this spot for New York Air's Super Shuttle Service had a single fact to work with. New York Air's Super Shuttle seats were 23 percent roomier than the famous Eastern Airlines shuttle seats. The public knew that Frank Borman, then chairman of Eastern Airlines, had been an astronaut, and that the crew's quarters in space shuttles had been very cramped in the years when Borman flew in them. The creative team based the commercial on that fact.

This focus let them avoid all the clichés of airline advertising. In addition, rather than dwelling on Borman's courage—the usual cliché of astronaut commercials—the copy focused the audience's attention on his discomfort during his ordeal. By changing the context in which the astronaut was shown, the creative team turned a cliché into an innovative, intrusive element that attracted viewers' attention.

Some ad people might write this visual off as borrowed interest. That would be a mistake. Borman had indeed been an astronaut, and he was appearing regularly in Eastern commercials as their spokesman at that time. And astronauts, as a group, have always had as much, if not more, to do with flight as airlines, planes, and passengers.

The contrast of the symbolic or metaphoric visual and the specific concrete facts—Eastern "offers a mere 475 square inches of room, but New York Air's Super Shuttle offers seats fully 23% roomier" made this commercial provocative—and focusing the copy on the facts helped make it convincing.

The tongue-in-cheek quality of the last line of the copy, presented over a picture of the astronaut literally standing on his head ("Now, just because Frank Borman flew like this, doesn't mean you have to"), helped maintain the friendly, sophisticated personality the agency's previous advertising had created for New York Air. It also accomplished something else, which was a bit more subtle but equally important in advertising terms; it helped make what was actually an extremely competitive spot seem more like a gentle, good-natured poke in the competition's ribs than an ungentlemanly, abrasive slam.

Notice, too, that the basic visual, which had great appeal, did not change in any substantial way for a full thirty seconds. It could have been dull if the art director had not helped to maintain visual interest (and added a whimsical, offbeat touch) by turning the film so the astronaut turned in the circle and wound up on his head. The result? First, the point of the spot—"greater comfort with New York Air"—was driven home sharply because the competitor's chairman was shown in the most uncomfortable position of all. Second, although there was just enough movement to keep the single visual interesting, there was not so much that it detracted from the copy.

Perhaps the most important and instructive of all the positive attributes of this commercial is that, even though it is subtle, powerful, and whimsical, and communicates powerfully in both explicit and implicit terms—it is simple.

ᏅNEW YORK AIR                    "BORMAN"
                                 :30 TV COMMERCIAL

ANNCR: Before he became the chairman of Eastern Airlines,

Frank Borman was an astronaut

and flew in some pretty cramped quarters.

Maybe that's why the average seat on Eastern's shuttle offers a mere 475 square inches of room.

But on New York Air's Super Shuttle, our seats are a full 23% roomier.

Now, just because Frank Borman flew like this, doesn't mean you have to.

New York Air
Super Shuttle Service

SILENT SUPER: New York Air Super Shuttle Service.

# CUISINART

What makes this ad for Cuisinart's steamer tops so successful is its provocative headline and tasteful, very simple layout. The headline has a double meaning, but it is not obscure. The first meaning, that this headline may enrage you, is provocative. The second meaning, that the ad may convince you to steam cook your foods, is relevant. The ad contains a lot of copy, the signature of the president, the name of the product, and a picture of two of the products—but it does not look cluttered.

Some people may not understand the headline at first glance. But I think most potential Cuisinart customers will. The advantage of a headline with a bit of word play that is both provocative and relevant, and is not cutesy or precious, is that it will lead the reader to make certain unconscious positive assumptions. He assumes clever ads with an up-to-date look are run by clever, up-to-date manufacturers who make high-quality, up-to-date products.

# ARBY'S

This Arby's ad, directed at potential franchisees, ran in newspapers, so an illustration was used instead of a photograph. A photograph would not reproduce well in a space this size in a newspaper. Since the copy is short, there is room for the logo, a headline in very bold type, and an illustration. The ad could have run without the picture, but the picture draws attention to the ad (as I recall, there were no other ads with pictures on the page on which this ad ran). The picture also makes it immediately clear that, in one way or another, the ad is about food, specifically sandwiches sold in restaurants.

The double meaning—Arby's on a restaurant "roll," and the colloquial meaning of "on a roll," successful—also helps draw attention to the ad. Most of the other ads near this one were quite "straight": They simply announced what the ad was about. Note that, as with most successful headlines using word plays, it takes very little effort on the reader's part to dope out both meanings, because both are relevant to the subject of the ad.

# EINSTEIN MOOMJY

Einstein Moomjy has run one of the liveliest and most successful print campaigns in the New York area for many years. This ad ran in newspapers early in 1988. It announces a sale, in a very provocative way.

The headline is provocative, of course, because the year 1988 has been converted into a carpet price. While "happy 1988" may strike you as a blind headline, it is not likely that many readers will be confused about what product is being advertised, because the phrase "a square yard" sits just beneath the large headline. The reader gets the joke immediately. And this joke is what sets this ad apart from and above the many other dull, straight, artless retail ad headlines in the newspaper.

The lesson here is that, even though you are advertising a straight-forward sale, there's no reason not to do it in an especially cheerful, interesting way—even when you don't have a lot of space.

Is a headline with a double meaning always the best way to make your small-space ad provocative? No. It might not be appropriate. If you were advertising a funeral home, for example, it's likely that word plays would not be well received unless they were written very skillfully. (A talented creative team was assigned an ad encouraging funeral directors to ship bodies aboard railroad trains instead of by jet, the way they usually do. The headline the team came up with: "Henry Always Hated Flying." The client, Amtrak, bought the ad and ran it, and the response among funeral directors was very positive.) Another example is classified ads, where space is extremely limited. In that case, in most instances, it pays to use direct, declarative headlines.

"Four Berbers, No Waiting" is a take-off on the old sign, "Four Barbers, No Waiting," which used to hang in barber shops before appointments became necessary. The word play is relevant because a Berber is a type of rug. The clever headline for this sale ad helps attract attention and the ad's witty quality leaves the reader with an implicit positive impression of the store.

"Einstein Moomjy Needs A Live Wire With Wall To Wall Connections." In keeping with the rest of their advertising, and with the store's upscale image, Einstein Moomjy decided to have a little fun with this ad for a contract salesperson. Every piece of advertising they do fits in with their plan to give readers the implicit impression that they are a hip, well-run store featuring high-quality, contemporary merchandise.

## DANCE ST. LOUIS

This small-space ad for Dance St. Louis' '85–'86 season was one of a series of similar ads in the local newspaper. The pun, set quite large, attracts attention. The silhouette of a dancer in the logo adds interest to the ad and signals its intent to the reader immediately. The copy is blessedly short and to the point. The fact that it contains only one adjective, which is unheard of in this sort of ad, makes it seem more dignified than if it were filled with encomiums from reviewers. This ad is proof that advertising for capital-C cultural events does not have to be stuffy, reverential, and dull.

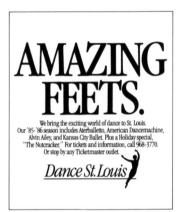

**AMAZING FEETS.**

We bring the exciting world of dance to St. Louis. Our '85-'86 season includes Aterballetto, American Dancemachine, Alvin Ailey, and Kansas City Ballet. Plus a Holiday special, "The Nutcracker." For tickets and information, call 968-3770. Or stop by any Ticketmaster outlet.

*Dance St. Louis*

## DENTAL IMPLANTS

One of the newest and most promising dental procedures is permanent implants that replace removable dentures. For patients who have the money (it can run into the tens of thousands of dollars to replace entire upper and lower dentures), implants can end the pain and embarrassment of loose dentures forever.

In many cases, forcing an agency to put the benefit in the headline restricts their creative freedom and tends to make your ad look like every other ad. In rare cases like this one, however, when you are selling a product that is unique and newsworthy, it pays to be as direct as you can be.

**Trade your dentures for real teeth.**

If you wear dentures or a partial denture, you should know about a remarkable breakthrough in dental care called "osteointegration," or "o.i." for short.

Osteointegration is a fancy word to describe a new way to replace your dentures with permanent new teeth. These teeth are part of a non-removable bridge fixed to the jawbone. They are not only as *comfortable and natural looking as real teeth, but actually stronger.*

This fixed, permanent bridge looks and feels natural. It is attached in a special way, at a point that is hidden below your lipline. Unlike removable bridges, it provides you with your normal chewing capacity. *That means you can smile, bite, chew, and eat corn on the cob in perfect comfort and absolutely without fear of embarrassment.*

How safe is "o.i."? This procedure was devised in Sweden, more than 22 years ago. Since that time it has been performed on nearly 10,000 patients, ranging in age from 14 to 92. The success rate has been an astounding 99%.

Dentists across the country are enormously enthusiastic about O.I., which they regard as the kind of breakthrough that occurs perhaps once in a generation. O.I. has enormous potential; it actually promises to end pain, embarrassment and discomfort completely for millions of denture wearers.

For more information about O.I., please call the American Dental Association. Or call R.D. Dental Associates, in confidence, at (914) 761-5500. Ask for Nancy.

**R.D. DENTAL ASSOCIATES**
80 EAST HARTSDALE AVE., HARTSDALE, NEW YORK 10530

It is harder than it looks to create an effective ad with a straight headline, even for a new and exciting product. Since this is a professional product, and the ad was signed by a dentist, the tone of the headline and the copy had to be confident but not strident or undignified. Since the ad was small and the copy had to be highly informative, the headline had to be short.

The ad had to have a restrained look, but it had to stand out from other ads as well as editorial matter. The double-ruled lines around the borders give the ad a distinctive, classic look and help isolate the ad on the page. The thin lines between paragraphs help make the copy look easy to read.

## UNITED TECHNOLOGIES

The ads in this long-running series for United Technologies do everything corporate ads should do and nothing they shouldn't do.

They are not filled with long-winded, flowery copy about abstract topics. They do not feature photos or illustrations of abstract, symbolic objects like clouds, skies, and disembodied hands reaching toward distant horizons. They do not contain photos of corporate chairmen, presidents, marketing directors, or boards of directors. They do not show clichés like conference tables, conference rooms, office buildings, or the inside or outside of factories.

Each ad contains a huge, stunning picture of something that every reader can identify almost immediately. The contrast between the huge pictures and the small block of copy makes the ads extremely provocative. The copy, which serves almost as a caption, promises the reader some useful information about the subject shown in the picture. Since there is so little copy, it looks easy to read. (Corporate ads filled with huge blocks of copy convey a kind of arrogance. They seem to say, "We feel we are important enough for you to take time from your daily routine in order to read fifteen hundred words about us simply because we are such terrific people.")

It is said that women infer a lot about a man's basic intelligence and effectiveness from the way he is dressed; the more fashionably he is dressed and the better coordinated his clothing, the more they think of him. The same is true of corporate advertising. The intrinsic quality of these large photographs rubs off on the company; readers infer all sorts of things about a company's capabilities and effectiveness from the look of its ads.

## ELIZABETH GRADY FACE FIRST

The Elizabeth Grady Face First ad would have worked well as an all-type ad, because the head-line is very provocative. But it would not have been nearly as appealing visually, nor would it have been as effective. The photo (the ad was printed in color) is more than a conventional and appropriate illustration for a skin care product. It makes the headline livelier and more vigorous than it would be without a photograph by providing a symbolic example of the kind of woman the headline refers to.

Sometimes a relatively conventional photograph or illustration is all that's needed to turn a highly provocative headline into an extremely effective ad.

## MISCELLANEOUS EXCELLENCE

The two American Express celebrity endorsement ads feature Eileen Ford, of the famous Ford modeling agency, and playwright Beth Henley. Neither of

Eileen Ford. Cardmember since 1960.

Beth Henley. Cardmember since 1982.

these two highly accomplished women has a famous face. The reader may be familiar, or at least vaguely familiar, with their names. The fact that they are not celebrities in the commonly accepted sense adds interest to the ads. The reader assumes he should know who they are even if he doesn't. The white space (it is actually filled with the American Express logo, printed very light) isolating each portrait draws attention to it. The brief, understated copy adds dignity and implicit snob appeal to the advertising.

The artful El Al Airlines ad uses a remarkably clever, highly relevant visual pun to draw attention to the message in a cheerful, whimsical way. Since this ad is clever and sophisticated, it sends the reader the implicit message that El Al is an airline run by clever people and chosen by sophisticated travelers.

The striking visual of a Sparkomatic radio literally torn in half makes this ad extremely provocative. I have discussed the ad in detail earlier in this book.

The Potato ad uses a delightfully whimsical headline–visual combination to attract the reader's attention to a serious subject. It proves that an ad doesn't have to be overly dignified and straightforward to be taken seriously. This is a good example of advertising that makes friends while it makes sales.

## NAMING NAMES AND USING QUOTES

These Peugeot ads are examples of excellent ads that name the competition without directly disparaging or "ashcanning" competitors. Readers don't expect ads for luxury cars to talk tough, so when they do, it must be done as it is here—felicitously. The tough but classy phrasing and the elegant sentence construction prevent the ads from sounding heavyhanded and offensive.

### IF IT WERE LESS ROOMY, LESS ATTRACTIVE, AND MORE EXPENSIVE, IT COULD BE A VOLVO.

If you're looking for the most cargo space you can get in a wagon, you owe it to yourself to discover what *Motor Trend* has called "the best kept automotive secret on the market today." The Peugeot 505 Turbo Wagon.

Its highly responsive 150-hp intercooled turbo-charged engine, incredibly precise rack-and-pinion steering, and vented front disc brakes not only make it one of the most enjoyable wagons you can drive, but also one of the safest.

So before you pay the price of a Volvo wagon, why not call 1-800-447-2882 for the name of the Peugeot dealer nearest you. And see how much wagon you can get for your money.

**PEUGEOT 505**
NOTHING ELSE FEELS LIKE IT.

### AFTER YOU TEST DRIVE A 180 HP PEUGEOT TURBO, YOU MAY HAVE TO TEST DRIVE A BMW 325. JUST TO CALM DOWN.

PRESENTING THE PEUGEOT 180HP TURBO S.

The legendary BMW 325. By many car enthusiasts it's regarded as the most exhilarating performance sedan you can drive today.

But were you to spend a few minutes on a test track behind the wheel of the new Peugeot Turbo S, you might well be convinced that the legend is riding on its reputation.

With a fully-integrated, turbo-charged engine that develops 180 hp and 205 lbs./ft. of torque, the Peugeot Turbo S would rocket you from a standing start to a speed of 60 mph in a heart-pounding 7.9 seconds. Pinning you to your infinitely-adjustable, orthopedically-designed bucket seat in the process. The less muscular 121 hp 325 would require a full 10 seconds to accomplish the same task.

Next, the Turbo S would whisk you through the quarter mile in just 16.3 seconds while the 325 would need more than another second to get you across the finish line.

Of course a car that puts this kind of power at your disposal (even the sound system features 200 watts of power and 6 two-way digital speakers) would be irresponsible unless it were designed to give you complete control over it. That's why the Peugeot Turbo S is equipped with fully independent suspension, precise electronically controlled, variable-assist power steering and, of course, computerized ABS braking.

The 505 Turbo S offers you a 5-year/50,000-mile power-train limited warranty and arguably the best roadside assistance plan available: AAA.* So why not call 1-800-447-2882 for the name of the Peugeot dealer nearest you, and arrange for a test drive. And see how you emerge from it a little too excited, you know what to do.

**PEUGEOT 505**
NOTHING ELSE FEELS LIKE IT.™

These two charming Volvo ads use headlines in quotes very effectively. Many advertisers erroneously think that because a headline is surrounded by quotes it is somehow livelier than an unquoted headline, but exactly the opposite is true. To attract attention, the headline must be well phrased. These headlines are actual quotes, but they are interesting because they are clever. Also, they are immediately relevant to car buying; in the case of the psychiatrist, the quote deals with the price of the car; the "Brownie" ad deals with safety.

Note that the photographs in these ads are conventional. An ad with a clever headline often does not need a clever visual. In this case, the conventional visuals help reinforce the ads' credibility. Basically, since each ad is an endorsement by a satisfied owner, a self-consciously slick, extremely dramatic picture, using lots of stark shadows, would neither be appropriate nor effective. These ads purposely have the warm, cozy quality of a high-quality snapshot.

# SOME GOOD EXAMPLES OF BAD ADVERTISING

## 17

One of the few things harder than creating great ads is creating ads as dull as those on the following pages. I never could have done it without a great deal of help from my good friend, art director Bill Weinstein. My hat is off to Bill; I have created good ads with many top pros, but I can truthfully say I create better bad ads with Bill than with any other art director.

To keep things simple, Bill and I dreamed up the Widget Company, which makes all kinds of products and sells all kinds of services. Each of the Widget ads we have created attempts to promote a different product or service—and each ad makes one or more very common mistakes.

## WIDGET AIRLINES

This ad features a photograph of a masterpiece, in this case Van Gogh's *The LangLois Bridge*. The aim is to convince readers that the airline offers such high-quality service that it is on the order of the quality of Van Gogh's best work.

This is an example of borrowed interest that doesn't work because it is far-fetched and forced. Artistic masterpieces have nothing directly to do with airlines; a painting is the work of one person, struggling to express a unique inner vision, while an airline is the work of thousands of men and women doing the same things again and again in a prescribed way.

In addition, this is a highly cerebral metaphor that lacks drama. The headline–visual combination doesn't tell the reader anything about the painting or anything relevant about the airline or the dedication, commitment, or competence of the people who work for it, the planes they fly, or the care the planes are given.

This approach is particularly unfortunate because it represents a missed opportunity. It takes the efforts of thousands of highly trained, hard-working people to make an airline work. Surely there must be at least half a dozen interesting perspectives and scores of interesting stories to tell about the results of these people's efforts to make their customers' travels less of a travail. Copywriters and art directors could use that information to come up with interesting creative concepts and headline–visual combinations that are more provocative than this one.

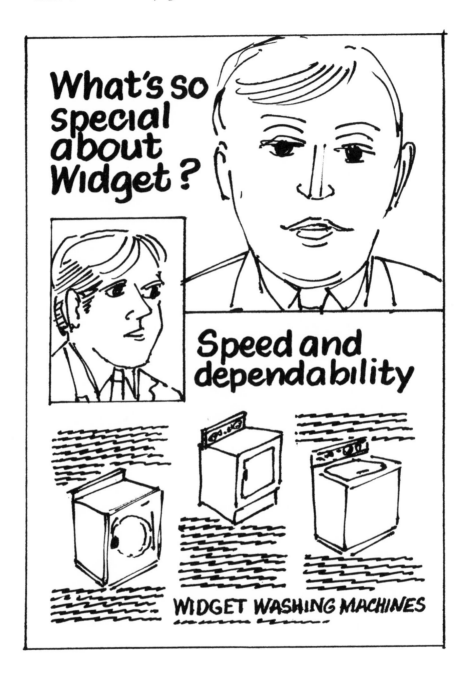

## WIDGET WASHING MACHINES

A headline that answers its own question is not interesting because it doesn't arouse the reader's curiosity or create a feeling of tension. Also, unless they are placed in a provocative context, ("What you don't know about speed in a washing machine could ruin your clothes"), abstract words like *speed* and *dependability* are not dramatic. One startling, specific statement about the speed or durability of these washing machines would have been more interesting.

Close-up pictures of two obscure, ordinary-looking executives are not interesting unless their pictures are accompanied by a provocative headline.

A good advertising photographer could make one large picture of one washing machine look dramatic, but even the best of them would have a tough time with three small pictures of three machines.

A washing machine is a fairly expensive, relatively complex item. Consumers want to know, in specific terms, exactly why they should buy your washer instead of somebody else's. A washer that works faster and is more dependable, even one that is fast and dependable but no faster or more dependable than anybody else's, is an important piece of equipment in any household. But these virtues cannot simply be laid out flat before the consumer, as a Persian rug might be. They must be brought to his attention in a dramatic way, which means you must place the benefits in the context of some sort of story. Failing that, you must make some sort of explicit, fairly surprising statement about them, or about the washing machines, that will catch the reader's attention immediately. In other words, you need a visual or verbal hook. "Speed" and "dependability" are too sterile and flat to serve as a hook. Simply naming those virtues in large type in an ad is like making a speech about them. When we try to create advertising that consumers will pay attention to, we are after the commercial equivalent of a play, not a speech.

## WIDGET SCOTCH

This is a perfect example of the "yuppies in the penthouse" approach to whiskey advertising. This headline–visual is not interesting because it is not dramatic. It is not dramatic because it is vague; it does not tell or begin to tell a story about the people in the picture. The question an advertiser must ask himself when he is shown an ad with a picture of this kind is, "Does the headline tell me who these people are and why the reader should be interested in them?"

The ads for Widget Scotch could attempt to create a relevant persona for the brand by making reference to actual facts or by alluding to situations in which the Scotch is used, or to occasions that are celebrated by giving the Scotch as a gift, and so forth.

For example, your advertising could refer to the fact that the buyer can feel confident and comfortable serving this Scotch to his guests because it's a quality Scotch for such-and-such reasons. If you elected to go that route, you would try to dramatize *the feeling of confidence or comfort* rather than use the actual words. Using this approach in your advertising may sound laboriously indirect if you consider yourself a hard-bitten, no-nonsense businessperson. But we all express ourselves in this indirect way in daily life. For instance, if you want your children to grow up with a healthy sense of self-esteem, you don't spend hours every day telling them how valuable they are and how much their very existence means to you. You express your admiration and affection for them by listening carefully when they speak, treating what they do and say with respect, and so forth. In other words, for the most part, you *act out* the fact that you hold them in high esteem rather than lecturing them directly, because you know instinctively that words alone won't work. As they grow, they incorporate the attitudes you acted out into their own psyches, and they grow up with the feeling that they are likable and worthwhile people. Since most advertising is about feelings or impressions of one kind or another, a great deal of the most effective advertising goes about its business in exactly the same way, using metaphors and symbols to convey meaning.

## WIDGET COMPUTERS

The main reason that this ad is not interesting is because it is vague. It does not tell or begin to tell a story, and it does not refer even indirectly to a specific benefit. The symbolic model for this ad is a speech instead of a play. It makes a flat statement instead of attempting to say what it has to say in an interesting way or enticing the reader into reading the copy by using an intriguing head-line–visual combination.

Why is Widget the choice? What does it have that IBM, Compaq, and Apple don't have? Five machines are shown. Like most people, I can't concentrate on more than one thing at a time. Which of these computers am I supposed to look at?

When your agency shows you advertising, before you look at each ad, ask your-self: "Once upon a time . . . what happened?" If the headline–visual combina-tion doesn't begin to tell you or at least give you a hint about what happened, it's probably a weak combination. A helpful statement you can make to yourself when you're evaluating advertising is, "I should buy this product because. . . ." If the headline–visual doesn't get at the reason even indirectly, chances are the ad is weak.

Also, since computers, like washing machines, all look pretty much the same, great care must be taken in computer advertising to photograph or illustrate the computer in a dramatic way. There are dramatic ways to photograph five com-puters on a page, but lining them up on an angle is not one of them.

Sophisticated advertisers may be impatient with my discussion of this ad. An ad, after all, is the end product of a lengthy, complicated thought process that begins with the marketing strategy. An advertiser may be inclined to say, "The hell with the ad. It's obvious that this ad is weak because the marketing strategy is weak—that's what we should be talking about." In many cases that's true. But quite often, even though the marketing strategy is perfectly sound, the ad-vertising is weak. In fact, many ads are so weak that you have to search through them to try to figure out the marketing strategy.

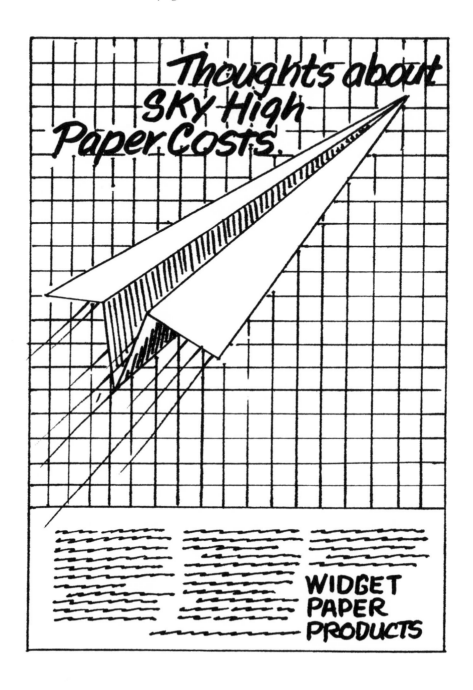

## WIDGET PAPER PRODUCTS

This is a good example of an ad with a fairly clever headline–visual combination, but no creative concept to speak of. A paper airplane in a paper company's ad is, or could be, a cute idea. The phrase "sky high" in connection with a soaring airplane is fairly clever and relevant to the picture.

However, the problem with all this cuteness and word–picture play is that, after having read the headline and looked at the picture, the reader still doesn't know what any of this has to do specifically with the benefits Widget Paper Products offer.

This kind of cuteness for its own sake is what many agencies mistake for creativity. The whole idea of this headline–visual combination, lively as it may be, is abstract and vague. If there was a lively, clever word–picture combination that referred to how Widget could save the reader money, or showed him how to use less paper or how to use it more efficiently, the liveliness and cuteness would have a purpose and the ad would be more effective.

This ad may seem too frivolous and vague on its face to be taken seriously by sophisticated advertisers. But literally hundreds of ads as weak as this one, and weak for the very same reasons, run in well-known business magazines—and hundreds of trade magazines—every year.

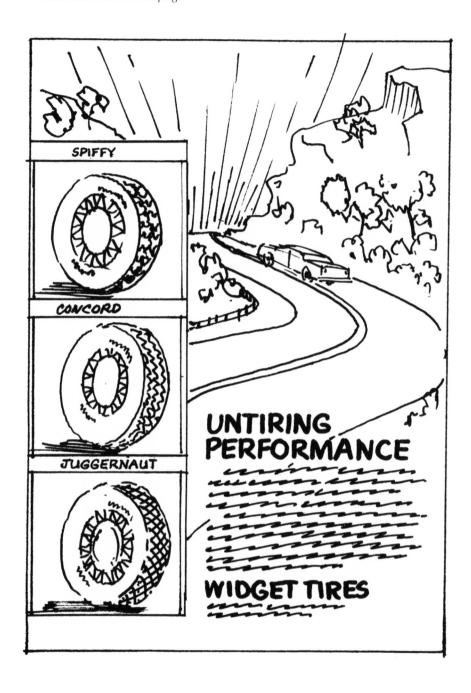

## WIDGET TIRES

"Untiring performance" is a clever play on words. Unfortunately, it fails to tell us or begin to tell us anything unique about the generic or competitive benefits Widget tires offer consumers. (Compare this headline to the headline I referred to earlier, "It Bites When Cornered." The "Bites" headline is more specific; it relates directly to the gripping power, or traction, that the tire offers hard-driving consumers.)

Tires are important, expensive pieces of equipment. Tire buyers probably care most about price and convenient retail locations and assume one heavily advertised tire is as good as any other. Nonetheless, to some degree, a prospective buyer expects a tire ad to reassure him that a given brand is worth buying. One of the best ways to do that is to use a headline–visual combination that says something specific about the tire or at least hints at some specific benefit the tire offers.

To everybody but car and tire buffs, one tire looks pretty much like another. So there's no reason to waste valuable space on three small pictures of tires. And pictures of similar size printed over a conventional picture of a car driving off into the sunset are not dramatic, especially with this headline, because they fail to tell us or begin to tell us a story. Finally, this ad is dull because neither the layout, the visual, nor the headline–visual combination contains any sense of surprise or of the unexpected.

## WIDGET DEVELOPMENT OF MISSOURI

Rhetorical questions do not usually make good headlines because they tend to be impersonal. Basically, most ads are substitutes for face-to-face, one-to-one sales pitches. When I look at an ad or watch a TV commercial, I should have the feeling that a single person paid for the ad and is using the ad to speak to me as an individual. When I look at this ad, I have the feeling that the fifteen-person board of directors who manage Widget Development of Missouri is standing on top of a high mountain, shouting down at me and a thousand other people in a valley miles below, through a bullhorn.

Also, I have the feeling Widget feels they can take their own sweet time explaining the importance of their company to the reader. In other words, this ad is dull because it tries to say too much, takes too long to say it, and says it in an impersonal way.

The four small visuals are not dramatic; they have a dry, sterile look. They remind me of the icons on a Macintosh computer screen, because they are didactic or symbolic rather than dramatic. They do nothing to help to personalize this ad. They also make this ad look like it's about four different, complicated subjects.

Widget Development's management has not grasped the fact that the most interesting advertising has much of the quality of gossip—it is direct, to the point, and, above all, personal and emotional. Widget might respond by saying there are certain companies that are engaged in complicated undertakings that can't all be described in quick, simple, personal terms.

I would suggest to Widget and any other company that feels the way they do about advertising that they rethink what advertising can and cannot do. If a company is engaged in many complicated undertakings, their advertising must sum up their activities in a simple, terse, dramatic way. If their advertising is dramatic in a generalized way, as United Technologies' corporate print campaign is, for example, it will leave readers with a single, strong, positive, memorable impression of the organization. The impression this ad leaves me with is that Widget is a big, dull company that I am not interested in, because it does a lot of dull, stuffy things in dull, stuffy ways.

This example may seem far-fetched, but the impersonal, unemotional approach it takes is very common, especially in corporate advertising.

To understand advertising is to understand its limitations. It cannot effectively convey long, involved, complicated messages to people; magazine and newspaper articles and books can do that effectively.

## WIDGET BANK

An important advertising guideline is: If your headline tells people something they already know, and you want them to pay attention to it, you must tell it to them in an interesting way. The headline in this ad says something obvious but does not say it in a particularly interesting way. And the second sentence, "We Can Help!," is both cumbersome and unnecessary (it is implicit that the advertiser whose name is on the ad can help the reader deal with change: why else would the advertiser pay for the space?).

Widget Bank management might insist that this headline merely reminds the reader that change is inevitable. That's O.K. But a great deal of space is wasted by attempting to depict the change that is in the wind by showing us an actual picture of wind, or its effects. If the customer is smart enough to understand the idiomatic expression in the first place, he's smart enough to form a mental image of change without the help of a photograph. A good headline–visual combination should set the story it has to tell in motion as quickly as possible; the advertiser should not waste precious time and space depicting something the reader can picture for himself.

The key question is: *How* can the bank help the customer cope with change? That is the thought this headline–visual combination should have attempted to dramatize, and which this headline should have attempted to put into words.

## WIDGET HOTELS

Headlines consisting of dull, flat statements, in quotes, make dull ads. Big pictures of obscure chairmen or presidents don't help matters much. Quoted headlines should follow the same guidelines as headlines without quotes: An ad is provocative when a quoted headline is interesting in and of itself or when it is combined with a picture in a provocative way. For example, an award-winning ad for Perdue chicken contained a large photograph of an uncooked Frank ("It Takes A Tough Man To Make A Tender Chicken") Perdue bird with the quoted headline, "The only tough thing about a Perdue chicken is becoming one."

Another reason this Widget Hotel ad is dull is because it celebrates the president of the hotel chain instead of the hotel. Consumers are not interested in hotel presidents; they are interested in the benefits the advertised hotel offers them that other hotels do not.

Many corporate campaigns, and campaigns for service organizations like hotels, banks, insurance companies, and brokerage houses, make the mistake this ad does; they assume that if their message is heartfelt and sincere enough, it will come across on the printed page. They also assume that if their corporate leader is a beloved and effective leader in person, his mere presence on the printed page will attract a reader's attention. That's possible, but not very likely.

Don't misunderstand me: There's no rule that says you can't show the company president or use a quote in an ad. It's just that a picture of the person and an ordinary quote is usually not very interesting. The person-and-quote approach is fine, but *it's only a beginning*. You must work hard to make the picture of the person and the quote you use as provocative as possible.

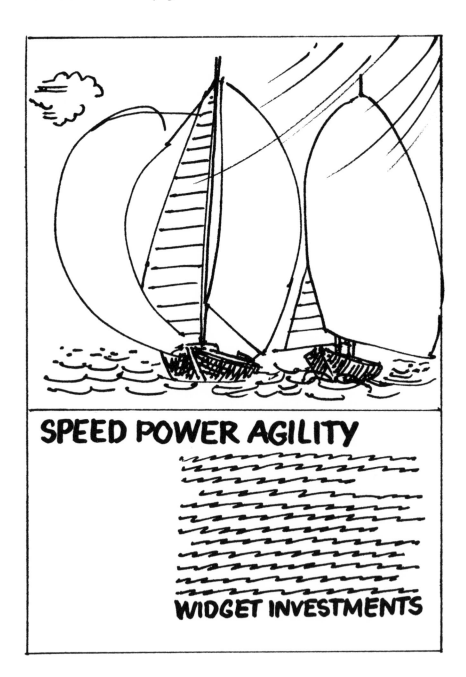

## WIDGET INVESTMENTS

Pictures used as metaphors for abstract characteristics such as speed, power, agility, competence, and honesty almost never characterize or define corporations very effectively. Why? Because the impressions these headline–visual combinations create are too diffuse to pique a reader's curiosity. Since they are vague and do not tell or begin to tell a story, readers do not find them interesting.

Remember my first-floor-of-a-department-store analogy? Imagine that you were trying to interest a passerby in Widget investments. You hold up a beautiful picture of sailboats under full sail, and shout at him, "Speed, power, agility!" He wouldn't know what you were talking about. He would be more interested if you made a specific, unexpected statement about the boats you're showing him, such as "These boats are made of cardboard!"

The less tangible the benefit the client's organization offers the consumer, the more important it is for that client's advertising to dramatize the point it is making by using tangible, concrete headline–visual combinations.

How can you make sure your advertising doesn't strike consumers as vague and diffuse? When you are called on to evaluate advertising, ask yourself the "once-upon-a-time" question. Study the headline–visual combination and ask yourself whether it answers the question, "Once upon a time—what happened?" In the situation pictured in this ad, nothing is happening except that the boats seem to be sailing or racing. The reader has not been given any reason to believe that the ad is about to tell him an interesting story about either boating or investments. If you train yourself to think of a print ad or a radio or TV commercial as a form of story that must be told, or begin to be told, quickly—a story that relates in some way to the benefit the advertiser offers the reader or viewer—it will help you avoid dull, fuzzy headline–visual combinations.

## SOME SPECIFIC GUIDELINES

1. Make sure that in your headline–visual combination, your agency uses simple, easily recognizable objects to convey, or start to convey, your message in dramatic terms. The subject or benefit you discuss in the ad may be abstract, but the words and pictures you use to persuade readers to read the ad should be concrete.

2. There are times when all-copy ads need what amount to decorative visuals simply to break up the dull gray look dense loads of type convey. But as a general rule, if a visual is merely decorative, you should change your headline. Try to find an approach in which headline and visual are integrated, so they act as a unit to intrigue the reader into reading the copy. Pretty pictures, or dramatic pictures of pretty things—sunsets, sunrises, sailboats running before the wind—that have nothing directly to do with your company, your products, your benefits, or your customers, make pretty, but weak, ads.

3. I hesitate to generalize on this matter because excellent ads can be written using subheads. But in preparing the work in this chapter, most of the ads we came across that contained subheads had weak, dull, or vague headlines. If your headline needs a subhead, ask your agency to try to come up with a headline–visual combination that says what it has to say in and of itself.

4. The weakest copy we came across was copy that was full of generalities. Do your best to make your copy lean and specific. Train yourself by reading *People* magazine and the *Reader's Digest.* Both are very well edited and enormously successful at providing millions of people with the kind of information they want or think they need, in easily digestible form. *People,* of course, is little more than a trendy, extremely profitable, beautifully packaged gossip sheet, but it is popular because it is edited artfully enough to make it seem like a *respectable* gossip sheet. Take note as you read it that gossip is never general; it is always about something specific and immediately identifiable. By the same token, copy is interesting to the degree that it is, or appears to be, about something specific.

5. Many of the hundreds of ads we studied in order to create the ads in this chapter *looked* great. They had photographs that were beautifully shot and the headlines used language in a lively way. Often, the headline–visual combination was artful and had a bit of zip—but the wit and flair of the headline–visual combination were useless because the execution lacked a strong concept. Even though your eye was attracted by the clever headline–visual combination, you had to search hard to figure out what the copy was supposed to be telling you about the company. The wit and charm of an interesting headline–visual combination must relate quite directly to what your ad is about, and what the ad is about should relate quite directly to the company and the benefits it offers the readers. Charming, pretty ads that don't get to the point quickly are like charming, beautiful people who have nothing worthwhile or interesting to say.

# CAN YOU SEE YOUR FUTURE IN THE STARS?

## 18

[open on B.L. in living room]
"HELLO, I'M BURT LANCASTER. I'D
LIKE TO TELL YOU HOW MUCH AT
HOME MY FAMILY AND I FEEL WITH CHEMICAL RESINS.
[move back to inc. table] TAKE THIS COFFEE
TABLE. [ecu table] ONE OF MY FAVORITES. [cut to B.L.]
THE FOLKS AT ACME CHEMICAL EXPLAINED TO ME HOW
IT'S NOT REALLY MADE OF BRAZILIAN ROSEWOOD
[cut to ecu small mounds of chemicals in his hand]
BUT A DEVILISHLY CLEVER MIXTURE OF RESINS,
LAMINATED GLASS FIBERS AND KEVLAR. [cut to cu B.L.]
YES SIR, CHEMICAL
RESINS BY ACME CHEMICAL. IF THEY FIT IN
WITH MY WAY OF LIFE THEY'LL FIT IN JUST FINE WITH YOURS."

Like a song or a series of vignettes, a celebrity, in and of himself, is not an advertising idea. He is not a creative concept. He is not a compelling execution. He is the raw material who may or may not be able to be molded into an effective advertising vehicle. If he's going to hang around in your advertising drawing attention to himself and away from your product, you should wait until your agency can offer you both a celebrity and a provocative way to use him, or get yourself a different celebrity, or give up the idea of using a celebrity altogether.

Celebrities tend to work best when they genuinely have something to do with the product, or when their public persona makes a "pretend connection" plausible for most of the audience. A pretend connection is one that is not necessarily literally true. The late Jack Benny, a generous man in real life, pretended to be extremely stingy in order to get laughs. Using him in advertising for a bank or a brokerage house, or using Joan Rivers, who supposedly hates to spend time cooking, in ads for microwave ovens, are examples of pretend connections.

From a marketing point of view, one of the best uses of a celebrity was GAF's use of Henry Fonda as a spokesman for their film some years ago. Fonda brought instant credibility to a film most consumers would have regarded as "brand X" without his endorsement.

Some years later, Doyle Dane Bernbach made excellent use of James Garner and Mariette Hartley for Polaroid. There was no connection between the cameras and the celebrities, and none between the two actors, although millions of viewers thought they were husband and wife. The memorable series of commercials was full of playful wisecracks and the kind of acerbic asides a long-married, affectionate couple would toss off. These spots brought celebrity endorsements to a new level of refinement.

Lee Iacocca's recent highly successful commercials for Chrysler are another example of both the creation and the excellent use of a celebrity. Earlier spots using Mr. Iacocca, made some years ago, were less than inspired. He was nervous and looked uncomfortable on camera. He did one spot with Frank Sinatra that many adpeople thought did both men a disservice. But today, after a tremendous amount of hard work on both Iacocca's and his agency's parts, he is a highly skilled performer. Chrysler has what may well be the most valuable advertising, publicity, and promotion property in the history of American business.

TV actor Bruce Willis has been featured in a series of successful commercials for Seagram's wine cooler. One spot I saw was shot in black and white. These commercials are imaginative, almost surreal episodes which, like certain beer, soft drink, and perfume commercials, appear to make no literal sense at all; they are an attempt to dramatize and project an attitude or personality rather than conventional product attributes or benefits.

There is something in the essence of Bruce Willis's performances in "Moonlighting" that millions of people find attractive and diverting. The heart of the Seagram's wine cooler campaign is this special essence Willis projects—Mr. Where-

It's-At; a hip, confident, knowledgeable, successful, self-mocking, supremely with-it dude who manages to represent the supreme embodiment of yuppiedom while failing to take the very idea of yuppiedom, or perhaps anything else, very seriously. Part of his appeal—but only part—is his looks, which seem to be half-way between handsome and, by Hollywood leading man standards, relatively ordinary. Whether or not the commercials themselves are your cup of tea, in their own way they help create a special sort of weird, wonderful, wacky, self-mocking, silly/sexy "Moonlighting"-type personality for the brand. The agency, the client, Edgar Bronfman, who is said to have personally selected Willis against the advice of his own staff, and no doubt Willis himself understood that a straight, stand-up product endorsement from Willis would be laughable. They had the guts and the brains to throw away the rule book in order to create commercials that take special advantage of Willis's unique appeal.

On the other hand, an actor like, say, Burt Lancaster possesses an entirely different kind of appeal. His is a towering presence; he is a classic movie star in every sense of the word. He has been with us so long, and has played so many roles so well, that we can't help but pay at least some attention to what he says. Be that as it may, an ad agency that wrote a fatuous script for him like the one that heads this chapter, and simply sat Mr. Lancaster in front of a camera and had him talk for thirty seconds, would be wasting his genius as a performer. It would be tantamount to making a movie of Lancaster reading selections from Sinclair Lewis's *Elmer Gantry* for ninety minutes behind a lectern on a stage, and asking people to pay admission to see that film. Lancaster's Oscar-winning performance in the movie came about because, broadly speaking, he was provided with precisely the right filmic concept and execution. That combination was what made magic happen. The same thing must occur to make magic happen in your commercial.

If you can get hold of a tape casette of the Seagram wine cooler spots, compare them to my mock script for Burt Lancaster. In a nutshell, that is the difference between simply using a personality in order to attract a random, fleeting bit of attention to a product, and building on a particular performer's personality and talent to create a memorable and highly effective piece of advertising.

There is another celebrity technique that is sometimes used quite successfully. Advertisers choose endorsers who have accomplished a great deal but whose names and faces readers and viewers are not familiar with, in the hope that the public will want to know who the people are simply because they're being used in ads. For example, American Express (see chapter 16) has used people like Beth Henley, a Cardmember since 1982, and author of the Pulitzer Prize–winning *Crimes of the Heart,* in its excellent celebrity endorsement print campaign.

Schenley Imports' striking Dewar's Profile series of print ads makes excellent use of magnificent black-and-white portraits of unfamiliar but highly accomplished people, with a color shot of the bottle and the whiskey in the glass on a table next to them. A recent ad featured Alessandra Ferri, principal dancer with the American Ballet Theater.

## THE BAD AND THE BEAUTIFUL

A rare few corporate presidents or chairmen possess the potential Lee Iacocca has; they can be turned into showstoppers. Most others, although they are perfectly attractive and capable individuals (one who comes to mind is Frank Borman, former chairman of Eastern Airlines and for years the centerpiece of Eastern's corporate commercials), seem to lack the necessary charisma to make an advertising campaign come alive.

Many times, smaller ad agencies sell naive, relatively obscure local advertisers on the idea of giving their products some glamor, and adding compensatory clout to a small TV budget, by hiring a celebrity endorser a bit past his or her prime. Often, the effect is exactly the opposite of what was intended. Instead of adding glamor, the contrast between the celebrity's former eminence and present obscurity underscores the anonymity and obscurity of the local product or service. Two plus two turn out to equal one, and both the celebrity and the product suffer.

It's hard to believe, but it still happens occasionally—the chairman of a huge company wants to tell his friends that he plays golf with this or that famous actor or nationally prominent entertainer. So he forces his agency to hire that actor for a huge sum and attempt to write effective commercials for him. This puts the agency in the impossible position of trying to make a dumb idea work as well as a smart idea would have. If they can't—and they almost never can—they're blamed for not being creative enough or for purposely sandbagging a good idea because it wasn't theirs.

I remember working on one very large account whose advertising featured one of the nation's most famous and wealthiest comedians. He had been a celebrity for decades. He and the client's chairman and the agency's management supervisor were golfing buddies. He insisted on being ferried to and from studios and locations exclusively by helicopter and limousine. On the set, he would talk directly to the camera, and he would move left or right a few steps, and he would hold up a product or two—but that was all he would do. Whether he was recording radio spots or TV commercials, he would do no more than a couple of takes. His diction was terrible, but nobody dared to suggest rerecording or dubbing. It was understood he would shoot only on certain days, only in certain places, and only at certain times, so everybody's schedule had to be arranged to accommodate his. He never failed to make it clear to everyone within earshot that he had better things to do with his time than shoot commercials, so the atmosphere on the set was always extremely tense and rushed. The constant compromises he forced everyone working with him to make made the campaign he was a part of, which ran for years, listless and dull.

Fortunately, in more ways than one, this type of personality is a dying breed. Younger, more hip celebrities see show business less as a calling and more as a business. Many of them take themselves far less seriously, and are more cooperative and accessible—and therefore far easier to work with—than some of the old war-horses used to be.

What does happen all too often, especially among clients who make a fetish of management by committee, is the hiring not of the best celebrity for advertising purposes, but the safest or most bland. Bland personalities tend to make for bland advertising, and bland advertising wastes money.

Unlike Bruce Willis, many extremely handsome or beautiful TV and movie performers who come alive in character turn out to be complete duds when it comes to pushing a product. The more earnest they are, the less convincing they sound. In contrast, certain performers—James Garner and Dinah Shore are two that come to mind—project a kind of pleasant amiableness and affability that seems to rub off positively on almost any product. Certain other very talented performers, especially comics, seem unable to lend much credibility to commercial claims or to foster or enhance viewer interest or involvement. This may be because so much humor is based upon unconscious, suppressed rage, and that rage seeps out between the cracks, so to speak, when the comic tries to project friendliness. Perhaps comics, who tend to be an insecure breed in the first place, can't help overpowering the product they're pushing simply because they feel they're competing with it for the audience's attention.

What applies to celebrities in TV advertising applies equally well to print. An effective testimonial print ad needs more than the mere presence of a celebrity. The ad must have some sort of creative concept or premise. A provocative headline–visual combination and tasteful and attractive layout will help the ad build upon the celebrity's inherent attractiveness.

It should be obvious that there is no sure and easy road to success with celebrity endorsements. There are simply too many intangibles, too many elements that deal largely or even solely with personality, to be able to make reliable predictions about who and what will work best every time and in every case. What can be said is that most ad agencies—most fairly large agencies, at any rate—have a great deal of experience in dealing with prominent people in all walks of life. Experienced agency producers and creative directors are quite hip about who is in and who is out, who is easy to work with and who is not, who has worked well before and who has not, and who is likely to work best in the future.

# LOOKING FOR AN AD AGENCY? MAYBE WHAT

# YOU NEED IS A CREATIVE CONSULTANT

## 19

There are two kinds of advertising consultants; ordinary, or conventional consultants, very often former agency account executives, and creative consultants. Broadly defined, an ordinary consultant is somebody who helps you find the ad agency that's right for you.

A creative consultant is a person who helps you judge the relative merits of competitive creative work from a number of prospective agencies. A creative consultant can also help you evaluate the work your present agency is doing for you. Contrary to what many smaller clients think, it is not true that only large clients can benefit from using either ordinary or creative advertising consultants. It may well be that the smaller a client is, the more he needs one or another kind of consultant.

Independent advertising consultants come in all shapes, sizes, and degrees of expertise. Each has his own perspective, his own credentials, his own way of working, and his own fee schedule. Since consulting is a highly confidential process, nobody really knows how extensively clients use consultants, or exactly how each one works.

Since creative consultants deal strictly with creative work, their methods vary according to each client's individual needs. They may spend as little as half a day evaluating a client's or an agency's work, take the afternoon to write up a critique of that work, and be on their way. On the other hand, a consultant who deals with the entire spectrum of an agency's operations may spend weeks with each client, especially if an agency search is involved.

My guess is that, no matter how each person operates, his method is likely to be an adaptation or a variation of the method outlined below:

*Step 1:* The consultant interviews your key advertising, sales, and marketing people. He examines the creative work that has been done for you in the past and discusses it with you. He discusses your relationship with your last agency and attempts to analyze what went wrong. Then he writes a detailed confidential critique of your past advertising, offering suggestions as to why it did or did not meet its objectives. That critique should also include an objective judgment of the structure and function of your advertising department, and his own judgment of exactly what the reason was for the troubles you had with your last agency.

The consultant should be paid a fixed fee for his time and for this report. Sometimes it can take weeks just to obtain interviews with highly placed executives in very large companies. In smaller companies, forty-five minutes or an hour with the president and another hour with the ad or sales manager is often enough to pinpoint the problem.

If you are satisfied with this report, at that point you can engage the consultant to help your company find an agency. Working this way has two advantages: For a relatively modest investment of your time and money, the consultant can learn what he has to know about you, and you can get a good idea of how he operates and how smart you think he is.

*Step 2:* The consultant interviews the most appropriate agencies, narrows the list in consultation with you, and selects the very best three to six shops to make final presentations.

*Step 3:* The consultant works with you to create a white paper spelling out everything the agencies need to know about your company and your advertising problems; the day, date, and details of the final presentations; and exactly what you expect from the agencies during the presentation.

He prepares a score sheet listing important categories and giving a percentage score to each category (professionalism, creativity, attitude, flexibility, chemistry, and so on).

Presentations take place in each agency's offices. Each agency has sixty minutes to present and thirty minutes for conversations and questions. No more than two presentations are scheduled for each day, but all presentations take place in sequence over a two- or three-day period.

*Step 4:* After each presentation, score sheets are tallied individually. There is a private, thirty-minute discussion period. Notes are taken.

*Step 5:* One full day after the last presentation, the final selection meeting takes place. Notes and tally sheets are compared, a general discussion takes place, and an agency is chosen.

I recommend that a client searching for a new ad agency use a creative consultant. During presentations of creative work, it can be difficult to determine precisely where the sizzle ends and the steak begins—to say nothing of trying to determine whether the steak is to your taste. A creative expert can offer you the kind of reasoned, impartial, objective perspective that can be extremely helpful.

## A MOST RADICAL SUGGESTION

In almost every case, when a client and an agency part company, the client blames the agency. If you are a client, this tends to prevent your people from seriously questioning what part, if any, your company played in screwing up the relationship. If something is wrong with the way your company handles its advertising, and senior managers avoid taking the time to ask some painful, probing, pointed questions, you run the risk of choosing the wrong agency and making the same advertising mistakes over and over again—and wasting millions, if not tens of millions, of advertising dollars.

I am not saying that every soured client–agency relationship is the client's fault. But some of them, perhaps many of them, are. What's more, even when the foul-up is primarily your agency's fault, you can still learn important lessons if you are willing to acknowledge the 10 or 20 or 30 percent of the problem that *was* your fault.

So what I suggest, which I am sure will sound absolutely hare-brained and goofy to many clients who read this book, is that the next time you are ready to fire your agency, you hire a consultant, preferably a creative consultant, to spend a couple of days examining exactly what went wrong in the relationship, and why. When it comes to advertising, it's the cheapest, fastest way I know of to root out any serious, long-term organizational or personnel deficiencies your firm may have.

If you hire a consultant the next time you break up with your agency, you may be out $10,000 or $15,000 tax-deductible dollars. But if the consultant is able to put his finger on a weak spot that you can strengthen, he may save you a lot of money in the long run.

If you tell me you can't spare the money for a consultant, I will tell you that means you can't spare the money to advertise. If you tell me you don't want to do it because nobody else does it, I will tell you that's probably the best reason to do it—because, as I made clear at the beginning of this book, 85 percent of the advertising all those nobodies are paying for is ineffective stuff that never should have seen the light of day. If you tell me you don't like being criticized, I'll tell you I don't either, but sometimes it's good for us.

# A MEMO TO THE CEO

## 20

1. The first three guidelines for creating effective advertising are:
   A. Keep it simple.
   B. Keep it simple.
   C. Keep it simple.

2. Remember that all advertising communicates implicitly as well as explicitly—and the implicit, unspoken, symbolic, or metaphoric communication is often the stronger of the two types.

3. Successful advertising makes friends while it makes sales. It makes friends by being tasteful, innovative, artful, and timely; by never, never insulting the reader's or viewer's intelligence or aesthetic sensibilities; and by being brief and to the point.

4. The heart and soul of your company, its personality and style and manner of looking at the world, should be reflected in every piece of advertising, especially corporate advertising, that you approve. If you don't have an agency you can trust implicitly to do that, find one you can trust and stick with them. If you don't seem to be able to find a shop you can trust, it may

be your fault rather than the agencies'. Talking over your experiences and attitudes about advertising with a consultant can help.

5. Trust your agency to show your executives their very best work the first time out. Don't play games with them; don't, for example, always make it a practice to kill the first batch of stuff you are shown just to demonstrate how tough you are and what high standards you have.

6. Your agency is human. They will make mistakes from time to time. Don't play Eric F. Berne's famous psychological game, "Now I've Got You, You Son of a Bitch." A good client–agency relationship is like a marriage: You must work at making it work.

7. Agency people are intensely involved with their work and get a tremendous kick out of doing a great job. They like to be appreciated. Let them know how much you appreciate their efforts. You have no idea how much good a small token from a person high up—lunch with the troops, a breakfast, a memo, a letter, a phone call from time to time, anything on paper with your name on it—can do for morale, and ultimately for the quality of your advertising.

8. Advertising can be created overnight, and mediocre advertising usually is. Don't force your agency to create yours that way. Give them as much time as they say they need.

9. Keep the advertising approval process streamlined. Hire the brightest advertising executive you can find and pay him what he wants. (If you want to know where to find him, look for a company whose advertising is excellent and hire the person who approved it or the management supervisor at the agency that created it.) Grit your teeth and give your advertising manager his head. Avoid letting your advertising become a political football by giving him complete political protection, especially from your salespeople. Obviously, sales, marketing, and advertising staff efforts must be coordinated up to a point. But once an advertising strategy is decided on, the creation and approval of advertising should be left solely to your advertising manager, his staff, and your ad agency. Some sales departments and the salespeople who run them are shrewd and sophisticated when it comes to advertising. But too many corporate salespeople who think they understand the ramifications of advertising in paid space, do not. They tend to think in the narrowly defined terms of prospects and customers and fail to understand the extra dimension, and the concomitant nuances and subtleties involved, when those prospects and customers are actually readers and viewers.

10. Give your advertising time to work.

11. Your advertising executives will take their cue from you. Make it clear to them that the way to get the best work out of your ad agency is to treat them

as partners, not supplicants or suppliers. It's easy to bully an agency. Don't. It doesn't become you. Ultimately, it will hurt your advertising.

12. Among the most valuable books your ad department can study are the yearly annuals of The One Show book (*The One Show: Advertising's Best Print, Radio, TV,* Volume 7 (8, 9, and so on), published in association with The One Club for Art and Copy, Inc. It's available in book stores or from The One Club in New York City.

The Advertising Club of New York, which runs the ANDY awards, produces an annual videotape of radio and TV award winners and a guide containing the winning print ads and campaigns. They're available, for $90, from: The Andy Awards, 155 E.55th St., Suite 202, New York, N.Y. 10022. The CLIO awards organization makes certain useful publications and tapes available for a modest fee. You can rent tapes of those TV spots that became finalists in each annual "CLIO Awards Show." The annuals put out by the Art Directors Club of New York (57th Art Directors Annual, and so forth) are excellent reference books. The Film Study Center of the Museum of Modern Art in New York City charges a small fee to watch their reel of "Seventeen Classic Commercials of All Time, 1963–1976." For less than $50, you can rent the 16mm reel from their circulating film library. The commercials are old, but they are well worth watching.

An excellent publication in which some of the best advertising photographers display their wares is *The Creative Black Book/Photography 1987* (1988, 1989, and so on), Volume II of a two-volume set. It's distributed by Friendly Press, Inc., 401 Park Avenue South, New York, NY 10016, and is available in art supply stores or from the distributor.

The more familiar your ad executives are with photography, and the more they understand the differences between good and bad photographs, the better judges of advertising they're likely to be. An excellent article about six very common shooting errors amateur photographers make appeared on page 24 of the January 1986 issue of *Modern Photography.*

It's a good idea to provide your staff with company-paid subscriptions to *The New Yorker* magazine. Make sure your people study the cartoons. To be effective, a good cartoon, like a good ad, must be simple, quick, clever, topical, and fresh. The best *New Yorker* cartoonists are part artist, part poet, and part social satirist; they not only make you laugh, they manage to suggest and comment on an entire style of life or milieu using only a few drawn lines and one or two sentences. What is especially valuable about them is that, like Ernest Hemingway's short stories, which I mentioned earlier, they communicate so much with so few deftly handled elements. And the best of them have a stylish, whimsical, highly contemporary quality that seems to give them a life of their own. That's the sort of liveliness you want in your advertising.

The point of having all this reference material lying around is not to turn your executives into creative geniuses. But it will help to create the kind of atmosphere in which the craft of admaking is taken seriously and admired. Unlike any other professional service you buy, the quality of the advertising you publish or broadcast is controlled directly by you. The more familiar your executives are with a cross-section of the most artful, stylish, and effective current advertising, the more receptive they're likely to be to excellent work.

13. When selecting an agency, use a creative consultant.

# NOTES

Chapter 1. We Have Met the Enemy and He Is Us

1. Tom Peters and Nancy Austin, *A Passion for Excellence* (New York: Random House, Inc. Alfred A. Knopf, Inc., 1985) 92–93.

Chapter 2. Lighting up the Heart of Darkness

1. Thomas Morgan, "War, Peace and Carl Mydans," *The New York Times,* Jan. 23, 1986, section 111, 19.

2. Ernest Becker, *The Birth and Death of Meaning* (New York: The Free Press Macmillan Publishing Co., 1971) 81–83.

3. Roger Manvell, *Chaplin* (Boston: Little, Brown and Company, 1974) 106.

Chapter 3. In Good Advertising, As in Marriages, What You Don't Say Often Says More Than What You Do Say

1. Ernest Dichter, *The Strategy of Desire* (Croton-on-Hudson, N.Y.: Motivational Publications, Inc. 1960) 124.

2. R.W. Apple Jr. "The Presidency: The Reagan News Conference: A Comparison," *The New York Times,* January 9, 1986, A20.

Chapter 4. Surprise!

1. Ann Cooper, "In a State of Grace," *Advertising Age,* January 16, 1986, 5.

2. Interview with Tom McElligott, *Inc.* magazine, July 1986, 30–35.

Chapter 5. News Is Almost Always A Surprise. But News Is Not Enough

1. Nancy Giges, "Mark's emphasis on creativity brings profits to Colgate," *Advertising Age,* April 20, 1987, 1, 87.

Chapter 8. Let's Not Be Quite So Literal

1. David McClintick, "Tales From the Fable Factory," *The New York Times Book Review,* 1.

2. Ann Cooper, "In a State of Grace," *Advertising Age,* January 16, 1986, 4.

Chapter 14. Must Reading for Everybody Who Has Anything to Do with Approving Advertising

1. Richard Behar, "SCF's little secret", *Forbes* Magazine, April 21, 1986, 106–107.

2. Russel L. Ackoff, *Management in Small Doses* (New York: Philip Wiley, 1986) 84–86.

3. Larry Reibstein, "For Corporate Speech Writers, Life is Seldom a Simple Matter of ABCs" *The Wall Street Journal,* June 30, 1987, 33.

# COPYRIGHT ACKNOWLEDGMENTS

Grateful acknowledgment is made to the following for permission to reprint previously published material:

"SCF's Little Secret," Richard Behar, *Forbes Magazine*, April 21, 1986, 106–107.

Ernest Becker, *The Birth and Death of Meaning*, (New York: The Free Press Macmillan Publishing Co., 1971).

Roger Manvell, *Chaplin*, (Boston: Little, Brown and Company, 1974).

Tom Peters and Nancy Austin, *A Passion for Excellence*, (New York: Random House, Inc. Alfred A. Knopf, Inc. 1985).

Ernest Dichter, *The Strategy of Desire*, (Croton-on-Hudson: Motivational Publications, Inc. 1960).

# INDEX

# ABOUT THE AUTHOR

**Dick Wasserman,** a well-known figure in the advertising business, is an award-winning copywriter at Levine, Huntley, Schmidt & Beaver, one of America's most creative advertising agencies. Mr. Wasserman has been writing advertising, consulting with corporations about their advertising, teaching copywriting, conducting creative seminars, and lecturing and writing about advertising for nearly twenty-five years. He has worked for many of America's top agencies, including J. Walter Thompson, D'Arcy Masius Benton & Bowles, DDB Needham, McCann Erickson, and Scali, McCabe, Sloves. He has written advertising for Volvo, Procter & Gamble, General Foods, Ford, Goodyear, Time Inc., Citibank, AT&T, Seagram, Xerox, Texaco, Campbell's, Gillette and RCA, among many others.

Mr. Wasserman's first book, *How to Get Your First Copywriting Job in Advertising,* is a recommended text in college copywriting courses at Iowa State, Pace University, and The School of Visual Arts. He lives in Westchester with his wife Barbara, a teacher, and his daughter Carrie.